ACKNOWLEDGEMENTS

Illustrated by
Julian Baker, Bob Corley, Dave Fisher, Mick Gillah,
David Graham, Stuart Lafford, Steve Seymour, Tony
Smith, Clive Spong, Roger Stewart, Brian Watson

Picture credits
12 Imperial War Museum
25 Imperial War Museum
34 Lockheed Advanced Development Company

*The Publishers would also like to thank the following
for their assistance*
Air France, France
Boeing International, USA
Books International, England
British Airways, England
Bundesarchiv, Germany
Canadair, Canada
Imperial War Museum, England
Lockheed Advanced Development Company, USA
RAF Museum, England
Rolls-Royce, England

Published in 1995 by
Vineyard Books, an imprint of
Andromeda Oxford Limited
11-15 The Vineyard
Abingdon
Oxon OX14 3PX

Planned and produced by
Andromeda Oxford Limited
11-15 The Vineyard
Abingdon
Oxon OX14 3PX

ISBN 1-871869-61-7

Printed by Graphicom, Italy

AIRCRAFT

Written by
Ian Graham

Vineyard
BOOKS

Contents

What is an aircraft?

An aircraft is a flying machine. Gliders, fighters, bombers, helicopters, airships and airliners are all types of aircraft. Indeed, so varied are today's aircraft and the tasks to which they are put, that it is difficult to believe that modern aviation really only began little more than 90 years ago. The fascination with flying has inspired mankind for thousands of years, and as long ago as the fifteenth century the inventor Leonardo da Vinci had designed flying machines – but it is doubtful whether they were ever built and tested.

Our story, however, begins at the start of the twentieth century when two American brothers, Wilbur and Orville Wright, made the first successful powered aircraft flight. From this achievement have come all of today's complex flying machines. In this book we look at a variety of the world's great aircraft – each one chosen because it represents a landmark in the development of flight. Because many of these aircraft were later modified, we often show more than one version to illustrate the variety of designs which were created.

FLYING THE FLAG
Many civilian and military aircraft carry badges and insignia. These are often based on a country's national colours, and are equivalent to the flags flown on ships.

Canada

Russia

Italy

CIVILIAN AIRCRAFT
Civilian aircraft are designed to carry passengers or cargo. The passenger cabins of large airliners are pressurised so that the passengers can breathe normally in the thin air high above the ground.

HELICOPTERS
Instead of wings, helicopters have long, thin rotor blades which whirl around. The spinning rotor blades enable helicopters to take off and land vertically, so they do not need the long runways that aeroplanes with wings require.

Rotor blade

Rotor mast

Console

Canopy

Aerial

Tail rotor

Tail fin

Propeller

Engine air intake

Passenger cabin

Tail boom

Engine

Rotor guard

Control column

Skid

Cockpit

Fuel tank

Aileron

Nose radar

Steps

Leading edge of wing

Cargo bay door

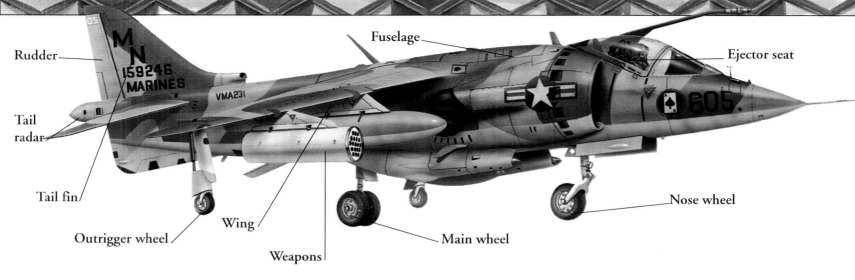

Rudder

Tail radar

Tail fin

Outrigger wheel

Wing

Weapons

Fuselage

Ejector seat

MN
159246
MARINES
VMA231
605

Nose wheel

Main wheel

MILITARY AIRCRAFT

Military aircraft perform a variety of different roles for armies, air forces and navies. Fighters attack other aircraft. Bombers drop bombs or fire missiles. Transport aircraft carry troops and vehicles. Reconnaissance aircraft spy on the enemy.

Elevator

Static dischargers

Exhaust nozzle

Engine

Trailing edge of wing

Navigation light

PRINCIPLES OF FLIGHT

All heavier-than-air aircraft have wings or rotor blades to lift them into the air, and all except gliders have engines to thrust them forwards fast enough to gain lift. Craft such as airships create lift in a different way, using lighter-than-air gas.

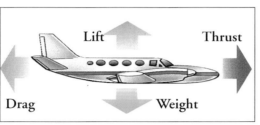

Lift

Thrust

Drag

Weight

LIFT, DRAG, THRUST, WEIGHT

Every aeroplane has four forces acting on it. Its engines thrust it forwards while air resistance, or drag, tries to slow it down. The wings must produce enough lift to overcome its weight. The diagram on the left shows these four forces.

PITCH, ROLL, YAW

An aircraft can turn in three ways, called pitch, roll and yaw. Raising or lowering its nose is a change in pitch. Lowering one wing and raising the other makes the aircraft roll. Turning the nose to the left or right is a yaw movement. The diagram on the right shows the parts of the aircraft which are operated to make the movements occur.

WING AIRFLOW

Air flowing over the top of a wing has to travel farther and faster than air flowing under it. This makes the air pressure over the wing fall, creating an upwards force called lift.

FLAPS AND SLATS

When a plane takes off or lands, slats move out in front of its wings and flaps stretch out behind them. They make the wings bigger to produce more lift when the plane is flying slowly. When it lands, spoilers lift up to "spoil" the wing's shape and reduce lift.

JET ENGINE

A spinning fan sucks air inside the engine, where fuel is sprayed into it and lit. The gases rush out of the engine as a jet, which produces thrust.

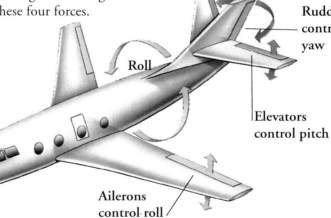

Roll

Yaw

Pitch

Rudder controls yaw

Elevators control pitch

Ailerons control roll

Airflow

Slat

Spoiler

Flap

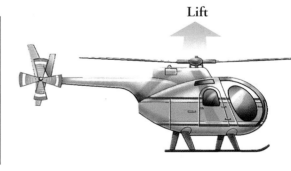

Lift

HELICOPTER

A helicopter's rotor blades are long, thin wings. As they whirl around, air flowing over them produces a force acting upwards. Making the blades spin faster or changing the angle of the blades alters the lifting force. The tail rotor prevents the helicopter itself from being spun around by the action of the main rotor blade.

7

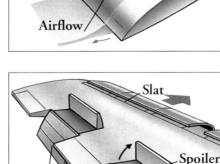

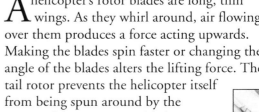

Development and uses of aircraft

The development of aircraft and the speed at which this has happened has been astonishing. Only 66 years separate the very first aeroplane and supersonic airliners. At first, a variety of purposes were achieved by a single aircraft. For example, the same plane was used for spying and dropping bombs. It became apparent, however, that one aircraft could not carry out different sorts of functions efficiently. Aircraft were therefore designed whose construction suited particular purposes. Nowadays, we have different types of planes, ranging from airliners and planes that spray crops and fight fires to bombers and spyplanes.

TAKING OFF

The chart below shows the key dates in the development of aircraft from the first plane in 1903 to the F-117A high-tech stealth fighter used today.

1940s: Avro Lancaster Bomber: the most successful bomber of World War 2.

1930s: First flying boats. These were planes that landed on water.

1947: First supersonic flight in a Bell X-1 experimental rocket-powered plane.

1936: Igor Sikorsky designed a helicopter with an overhead main rotor and a smaller tail rotor.

1930s: Development of airships. The *Hindenburg* (1936) was the largest of these.

1920s: First commercial airliner: Handley Page HP42.

1903: First powered aeroplane: *Flyer 1*.

Harrier AV8-A instrument panel

Sopwith Camel pilot

"Blackbird" pilot

Flyer 1's controls

DEVELOPMENT

Designers have constantly looked for ways of improving their aircraft. Aircraft have become safer, more comfortable and faster. As aircraft have become more specialised, so too has their design. Each new design has provided valuable experience that has led to further improvements.

FLYING CONTROLS

Cables were used to steer early planes. They were linked to the plane's control surfaces and were operated by the pilot. Nowadays, planes are too powerful and fast to be operated manually. In the latest steering system, called fly-by-wire, computers operate the plane's control surfaces.

Sopwith Camel wings

CLOTHING

Clothing worn by pilots has become more specialised. The pilots of early planes wore leather helmets, fleece-lined leather coats, trousers and goggles. Nowadays, pilots who fly at high altitude wear pressure suits and helmets.

Harrier AV8-A engine

Flyer 1 engine

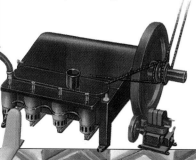

WINGS

The first aircraft had two pairs of wings held in place by wires and wooden struts. As aeroplane speed increased, the wood and wire caused too much air resistance. Modern aircraft have one pair of metal wings. The wings are swept back to reduce air resistance.

Concorde "delta" wing

ENGINES

The first aeroplane engines were piston engines, similar to those in a modern car. In the 1930s, Britain and Germany both developed a new type of engine – the jet engine. Jet-engine aircraft can fly higher and faster than piston-engine planes.

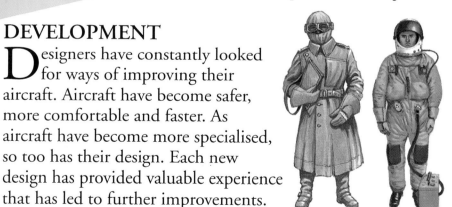

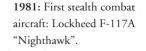

1967: First aircraft capable of vertical take-off and landing, as well as short take-off and landing: the Harrier "Jump Jet".

1981: First stealth combat aircraft: Lockheed F-117A "Nighthawk".

1949: First jet airliner: de Havilland Comet. Entered service in 1952.

1958: First transatlantic jet airliner services between London and New York with a de Havilland Comet 4.

1964: First stealth aircraft: Lockheed SR-71 "Blackbird".

1969: First supersonic airliner: Concorde.

USES

Aircraft are used for civilian and military purposes. They transport people and goods from place to place far more quickly than would be possible by road, rail or sea. Military aircraft are used for defence and attack. Some of them are bombers, others are fighters, others are capable of both. Some military aircraft are used for spying. Large numbers of small aircraft are also flown for leisure.

CIVILIAN AIRCRAFT

Holidays in far-away places would be impossible for most people without fast air travel. Business around the world would also be far more difficult. At first, there were very few airports. Aeroplanes took off from fields. Nowadays, many cities have at least one airport. The picture above shows the boarding walkway leading from the airport terminal to the aircraft.

FLYING FOR FUN

Many different types of aircraft exist that are flown for fun. Examples of these are balloons, single-seat aircraft called microlights, hang-gliders and gliders. Gliders, shown above, are first towed into the sky by another plane or by a winch on the ground, and then use rising columns of air to carry them upwards.

MILITARY AIRCRAFT

Winning control of the air is a vital part of winning a war. Fighters patrol the skies ready to attack enemy aircraft. Ground-attack aircraft and bombers strike against targets on the ground. Transport aircraft carry troops, vehicles and supplies to where they are needed and reconnaissance aircraft spy on the enemy. The picture to the right shows a jeep driving out of a Boeing Vertol CH-47 Chinook.

The first flight

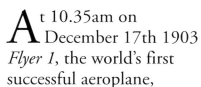

Wilbur Wright *Orville Wright*

At 10.35am on December 17th 1903 *Flyer 1*, the world's first successful aeroplane, accelerated along its launching rail and rose into the air.

WRIGHT BROTHERS

The first successful aeroplanes were designed by two American bicycle makers, Wilbur (1867-1912) and Orville (1871-1948) Wright.

Twelve seconds later, it landed 30 metres away on the soft sand at Kill Devil Hills near Kitty Hawk in North Carolina, USA. It was the first time a piloted machine had taken off under its own power and made a controlled flight. The pilot, Orville Wright, and his brother, Wilbur, had built the plane after four years of experiments with kites and gliders. Flying the first aeroplane was difficult and dangerous. *Flyer 1* had no cockpit or even a seat to sit on! The pilot lay on the lower wing and steered by sliding from side to side. It landed on skids, not wheels.

STEERING

Flyer 1 was steered by twisting its wings. The Wright Brothers called it wing-warping. The wings were warped, or twisted, by pulling cables attached to them and to the cradle the pilot lay in. The pilot steered by sliding his body to one side or the other.

Upper wing

Bracing wire

TAKE-OFF

While one brother piloted the plane, the other brother stayed at the take-off point and timed the flight with a stop-watch.

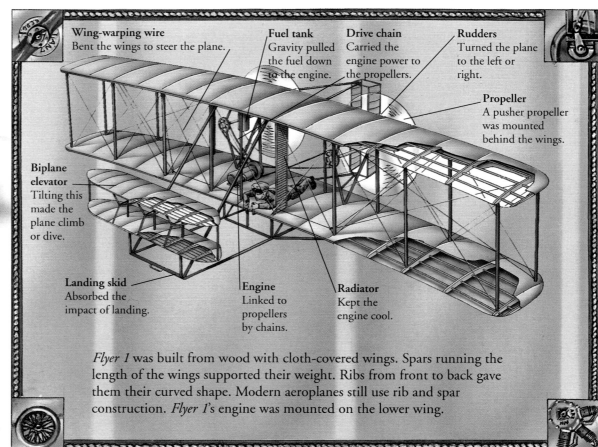

Wing-warping wire
Bent the wings to steer the plane.

Fuel tank
Gravity pulled the fuel down to the engine.

Drive chain
Carried the engine power to the propellers.

Rudders
Turned the plane to the left or right.

Propeller
A pusher propeller was mounted behind the wings.

Biplane elevator
Tilting this made the plane climb or dive.

Landing skid
Absorbed the impact of landing.

Engine
Linked to propellers by chains.

Radiator
Kept the engine cool.

Flyer 1 was built from wood with cloth-covered wings. Spars running the length of the wings supported their weight. Ribs from front to back gave them their curved shape. Modern aeroplanes still use rib and spar construction. *Flyer 1*'s engine was mounted on the lower wing.

ENGINEERING SUCCESS

The brothers designed their own engine because car engines were too heavy and motorcycle engines were not powerful enough. Their engine had four cylinders, weighed 90 kilograms and created 12 horsepower – about a sixth of the engine power of a small modern car. The plane's top speed was 48 kilometres per hour.

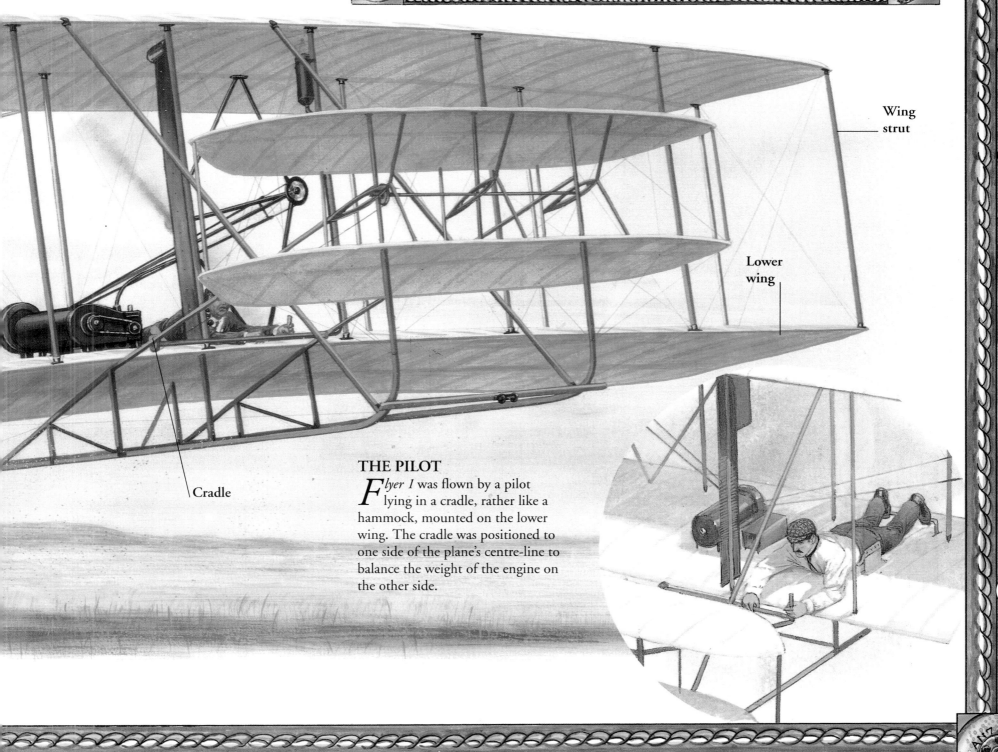

Wing strut

Lower wing

Cradle

THE PILOT

Flyer 1 was flown by a pilot lying in a cradle, rather like a hammock, mounted on the lower wing. The cradle was positioned to one side of the plane's centre-line to balance the weight of the engine on the other side.

Canvas and string

The Sopwith Camel was built during World War 1 (1914-1918) as a fighter plane, and was based on the earlier Sopwith Pup fighter. It was one of the greatest fighter aircraft of the war. At a height of 5,800 metres it could reach a speed of 185 kilometres per hour, and could fly 160 kilometres before it needed to be refuelled. It could fly for two hours at the most. More than 5,000 were built and they shot down almost 2,800 enemy planes. The Camels were faster and more manoeuvrable than most other fighters. But they were difficult to fly because the engine was very powerful for such a small plane. A careless tug on the joystick could send a Camel into a dangerous spin or even throw the pilot out of the cockpit. And during this time, pilots did not wear parachutes! The pilot sat in a wicker seat in front of the fuel tank. His view was restricted by the upper wing and struts.

HAND BOMBING

The Sopwith Camel carried four 11-kilogram bombs as well as other weapons. At the beginning of the war, before the introduction of bomb racks and aiming sights, the bombs were dropped from the cockpit by the pilot.

Bracing wire

Upper wing

Rotary engine

Lower wing

Wooden propeller

Metal engine cover

AERIAL PHOTOGRAPHY

Using planes for reconnaissance purposes was a new development in warfare. Sopwith Camel pilots took aerial photographs of enemy territory (1), and the photographs were used to make maps (2). These enabled the pilots to identify targets and the position of enemy troops.

① ②

PILOTS' CLOTHING

The air temperature drops very quickly as aircraft climb. Camel pilots had to wear leather helmets and fleece-lined leather clothes on top of thick jumpers, trousers, gloves and socks. Goggles protected the pilots' eyes from cold wind and from oil sprayed out by the engine. By the end of the war, pilots wore one-piece waxed-cotton flying suits lined with silk and fur.

DOGFIGHT

During World War 1, pilots on both sides became expert at dogfighting. The Sopwith Camel was especially good at this because it was so manoeuvrable. But the pilot with the most "hits" was the legendary German, Manfred von Richthofen, who was known as the "Red Baron" because he liked to fly a bright red Fokker triplane. He was eventually shot down and killed by Sopwith Camels in 1918.

Pilot's seat
A wicker seat, because wicker could bend and absorb the stresses of flight.

Fuel tank
The fuel tank was immediately behind the pilot.

Guns
Twin machine-guns on the nose fired between the propeller blades.

Engine
The Camel was powered by a 130hp Clerget engine, or a 150hp Bentley engine.

Rear spar
One of two main wooden beams that supported each wing.

Like other World War 1 fighters, the Sopwith Camel was built from a wooden frame with a canvas-covered fuselage. The plane was 5.7m long, with a wingspan of 8.5m. It had a maximum take-off weight of 672kg.

Roundel

Registration code

Wing strut

Tail skid

Fixed undercarriage

PROPELLER CANNON

The Camel below was fitted with a 37-millimetre Hotchkiss cannon firing through its propeller shaft. Some Camels had an extra machine-gun fitted to the top wing. Others had rockets mounted on the wing struts for attacking airships.

COCKPIT AND GUNS

Most Camels were armed with two machine-guns mounted on top of the engine in front of the cockpit. The guns could not swivel, so the plane had to be turned until they pointed at their target.

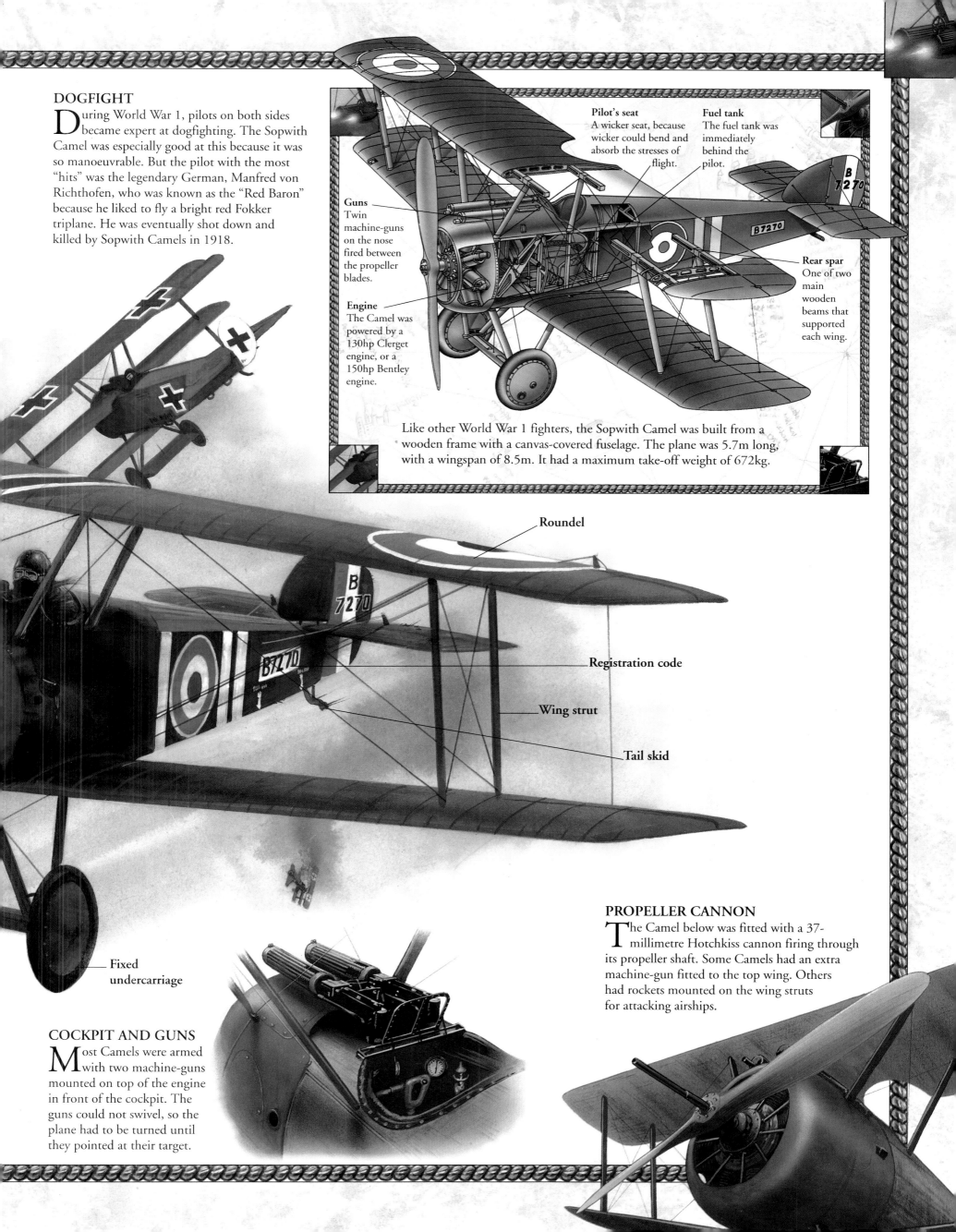

Flying banana

"It's so slow that passengers have ample time for breakfast, lunch and tea on the way to Paris!"
J.L. Dickinson, a passenger writing in 1932

The Handley Page HP42s were nicknamed "Flying Bananas" because of the curve in their fuselage. They were designed in the late 1920s initially as special air mail planes for the British Imperial Airways airline. The HP42s also met the growing need for commercial passenger planes, and became the world's first airliners. The routes took passengers from Croydon airport in London to France, India and southern Africa. Only eight of these biplanes were ever built. However, by the time they went out of service in 1940, they had flown a total of 16 million kilometres without injuring a single passenger. The HP42s were designed for comfort and safety, not speed. They flew at no more than 152 kilometres per hour.

CROSSING CONTINENTS

All HP42 flights took off from Croydon airport in England. The four-hour journey to France ended at Le Bourget airport, Paris. The six-day journey to India took passengers around the Mediterranean, through the Persian Gulf and over the sea to Pakistan. Another route flew over the Mediterranean and on to southern Africa. This took eight and a half days.

Wire bracing

Fabric wing-panel covering

Biplane tail

BOARDING PASSENGERS

Passengers boarded the HP42 through a canvas tunnel. As the plane was dedicated to the comfort and convenience of the passengers, the engines were started before they boarded to save time. The tunnel therefore shielded them from the backwash (wind) made by the propellers.

LOADING THE MAIL

Mailbags were loaded on board the HP42 at Croydon airport. The HP42 was designed as a mail plane because Imperial Airways needed a new plane to carry air mail to India. It was one of the first planes to carry mail on international scheduled air services.

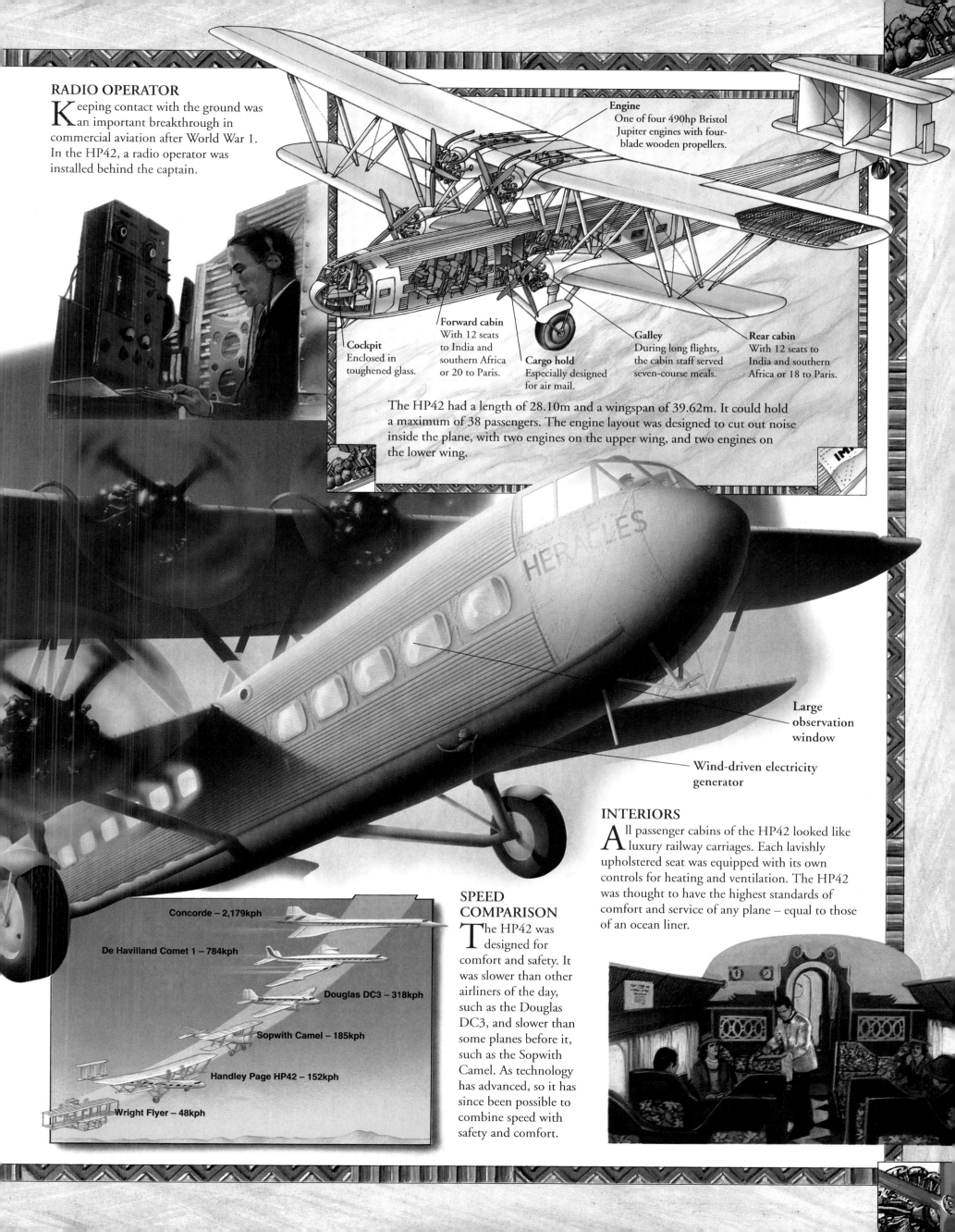

RADIO OPERATOR

Keeping contact with the ground was an important breakthrough in commercial aviation after World War 1. In the HP42, a radio operator was installed behind the captain.

Engine
One of four 490hp Bristol Jupiter engines with four-blade wooden propellers.

Cockpit
Enclosed in toughened glass.

Forward cabin
With 12 seats to India and southern Africa or 20 to Paris.

Cargo hold
Especially designed for air mail.

Galley
During long flights, the cabin staff served seven-course meals.

Rear cabin
With 12 seats to India and southern Africa or 18 to Paris.

The HP42 had a length of 28.10m and a wingspan of 39.62m. It could hold a maximum of 38 passengers. The engine layout was designed to cut out noise inside the plane, with two engines on the upper wing, and two engines on the lower wing.

Large observation window

Wind-driven electricity generator

INTERIORS

All passenger cabins of the HP42 looked like luxury railway carriages. Each lavishly upholstered seat was equipped with its own controls for heating and ventilation. The HP42 was thought to have the highest standards of comfort and service of any plane – equal to those of an ocean liner.

SPEED COMPARISON

The HP42 was designed for comfort and safety. It was slower than other airliners of the day, such as the Douglas DC3, and slower than some planes before it, such as the Sopwith Camel. As technology has advanced, so it has since been possible to combine speed with safety and comfort.

Concorde – 2,179kph

De Havilland Comet 1 – 784kph

Douglas DC3 – 318kph

Sopwith Camel – 185kph

Handley Page HP42 – 152kph

Wright Flyer – 48kph

Airship

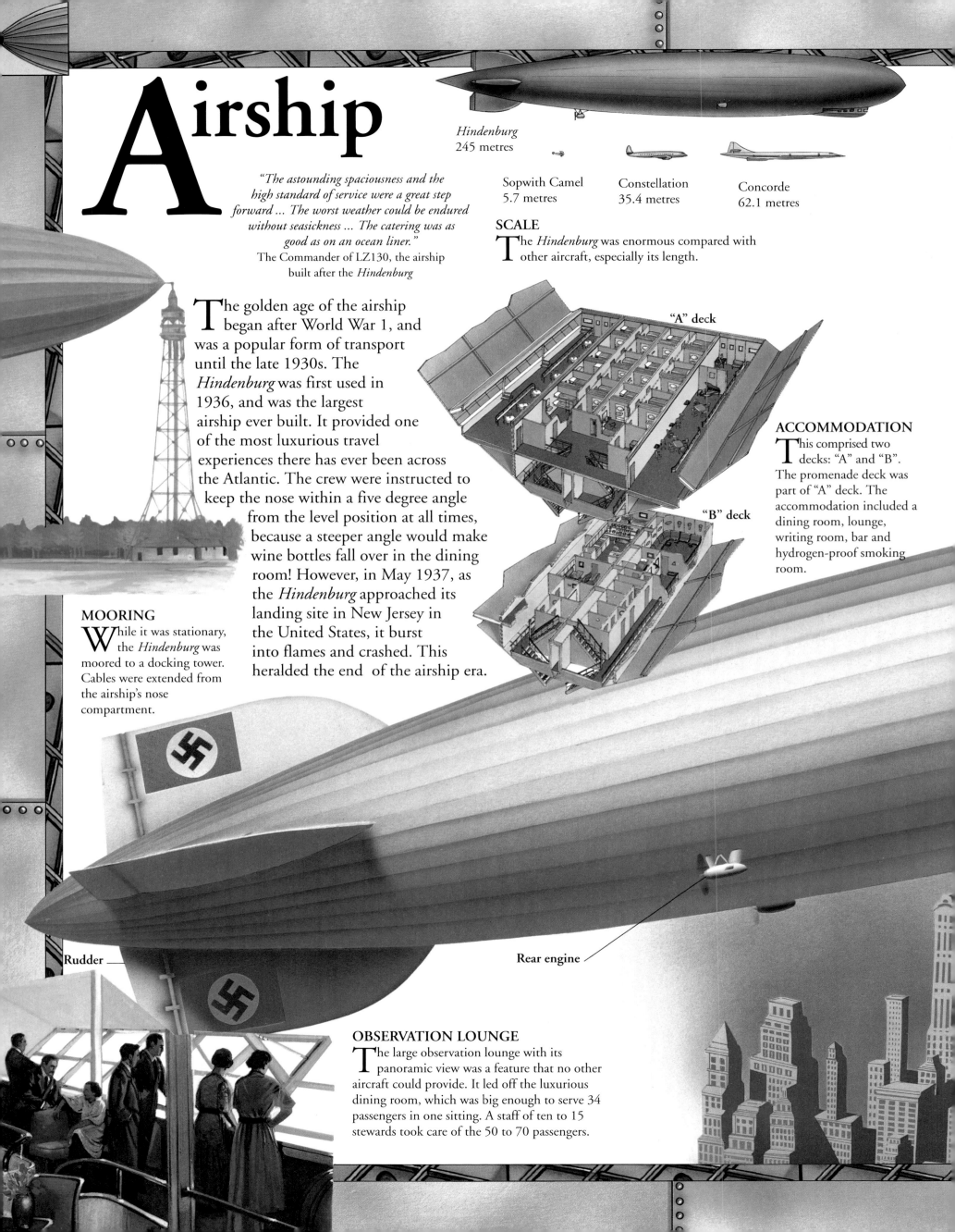

Hindenburg
245 metres

"The astounding spaciousness and the high standard of service were a great step forward ... The worst weather could be endured without seasickness ... The catering was as good as on an ocean liner."
The Commander of LZ130, the airship built after the *Hindenburg*

Sopwith Camel
5.7 metres

Constellation
35.4 metres

Concorde
62.1 metres

SCALE
The *Hindenburg* was enormous compared with other aircraft, especially its length.

The golden age of the airship began after World War 1, and was a popular form of transport until the late 1930s. The *Hindenburg* was first used in 1936, and was the largest airship ever built. It provided one of the most luxurious travel experiences there has ever been across the Atlantic. The crew were instructed to keep the nose within a five degree angle from the level position at all times, because a steeper angle would make wine bottles fall over in the dining room! However, in May 1937, as the *Hindenburg* approached its landing site in New Jersey in the United States, it burst into flames and crashed. This heralded the end of the airship era.

"A" deck

"B" deck

ACCOMMODATION
This comprised two decks: "A" and "B". The promenade deck was part of "A" deck. The accommodation included a dining room, lounge, writing room, bar and hydrogen-proof smoking room.

MOORING
While it was stationary, the *Hindenburg* was moored to a docking tower. Cables were extended from the airship's nose compartment.

Rudder

Rear engine

OBSERVATION LOUNGE
The large observation lounge with its panoramic view was a feature that no other aircraft could provide. It led off the luxurious dining room, which was big enough to serve 34 passengers in one sitting. A staff of ten to 15 stewards took care of the 50 to 70 passengers.

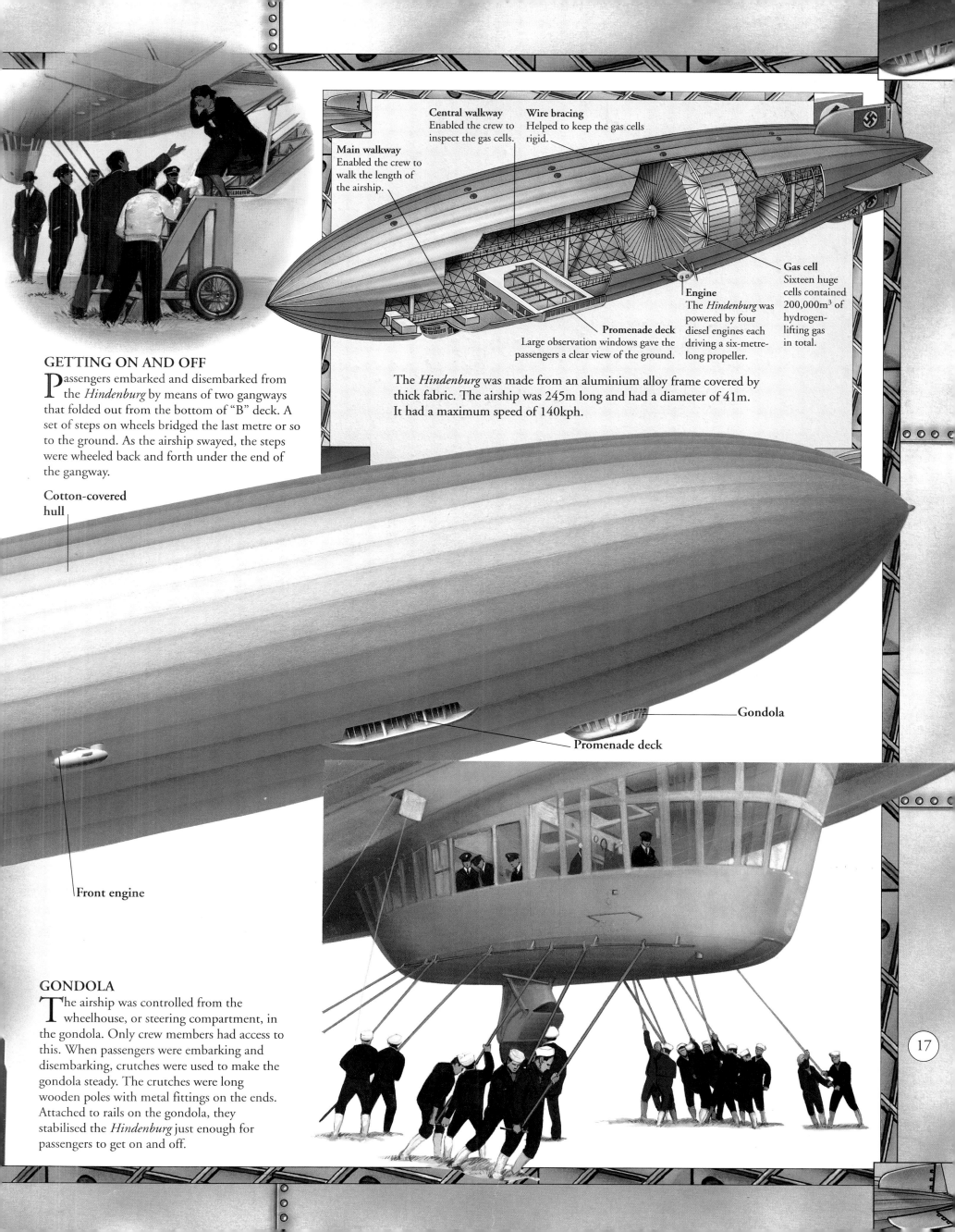

Central walkway
Enabled the crew to inspect the gas cells.

Wire bracing
Helped to keep the gas cells rigid.

Main walkway
Enabled the crew to walk the length of the airship.

Gas cell
Sixteen huge cells contained 200,000m³ of hydrogen-lifting gas in total.

Engine
The *Hindenburg* was powered by four diesel engines each driving a six-metre-long propeller.

Promenade deck
Large observation windows gave the passengers a clear view of the ground.

The *Hindenburg* was made from an aluminium alloy frame covered by thick fabric. The airship was 245m long and had a diameter of 41m. It had a maximum speed of 140kph.

GETTING ON AND OFF

Passengers embarked and disembarked from the *Hindenburg* by means of two gangways that folded out from the bottom of "B" deck. A set of steps on wheels bridged the last metre or so to the ground. As the airship swayed, the steps were wheeled back and forth under the end of the gangway.

Cotton-covered hull

Front engine

Gondola

Promenade deck

GONDOLA

The airship was controlled from the wheelhouse, or steering compartment, in the gondola. Only crew members had access to this. When passengers were embarking and disembarking, crutches were used to make the gondola steady. The crutches were long wooden poles with metal fittings on the ends. Attached to rails on the gondola, they stabilised the *Hindenburg* just enough for passengers to get on and off.

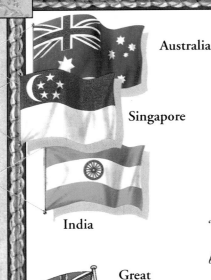

Australia

Singapore

India

Great
Britain

Flying boat

"I had a wonderful flight – taking off and landing in water was so smooth and fast! My journey to Marseilles was rather chilly, but the steward brought us blankets and hot Bovril. I landed in Australia, two weeks after leaving England, wishing my adventure could begin all over again."
Lady Geraldine Marshall, on her arrival in Australia with Qantas Empire Airways flying boat

SERVING FOOD

The Empire flying boat was equipped with a galley, or kitchen, where simple meals and drinks were prepared. At a cruising height of 1,500 metres, the aircraft could be shaken by sudden rough weather, making it difficult to serve meals and uncomfortable to eat them.

FLAGS

When the plane landed and became a boat, it often flew flags in the same way as a boat. The national flags of countries the plane visited or the merchant navy red ensign were above the cockpit.

Flying boats were developed in the 1930s and were the most comfortable and spacious passenger planes of the time. Their boat-like hulls and under-wing floats enabled them to operate from the sea, lakes and rivers at a time when there were few airports. Flying boats flew all the way to the Far East, making stops in dozens of strange and exotic places and taking about two weeks to get there. The Short S-23 "C" Class Empire flying boat was designed by Short Brothers of Belfast. The first of this class, *Canopus,* had its maiden flight on July 4th 1936. It was bigger, faster and more powerful than other flying boats. It carried airmail bags, light freight and 24 passengers.

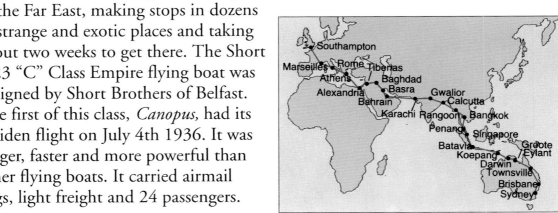

Southampton
Marseilles · Rome · Tiberias
Athens · Baghdad
Alexandria · Basra
Bahrain · Gwalior
Karachi · Calcutta
Rangoon · Bangkok
Penang · Singapore
Batavia · Groote
Koepang · Eylant
Darwin
Townsville
Brisbane
Sydney

THE EMPIRE ROUTE

Passengers boarded their flying boat at Southampton on the south coast of England. From there, they flew along the route shown on the map (left) to Sydney, Australia. The return fare for the journey was £274.

GETTING ON AND OFF

Passengers boarded their flying boat from a jetty, or floating walkway, to which the plane was moored. In the course of their journey to the other side of the world, they had to make frequent landings so that the plane could be refuelled. Each time it touched down, the passengers were taken ashore by launch for a meal or an overnight stay in a nearby hotel.

Navigation light

International identification number

All-metal wing

PROMENADE CABIN

Ocean-going liners often had a promenade deck where passengers could walk about and enjoy the view. The Empire flying boats competed directly with these liners and so they tried to offer a similar level of comfort and facilities. They had a roomy promenade cabin that enabled passengers to walk around and enjoy a spectacular bird's-eye view. They could see the ground below through observation ports.

Smoking lounge
There were seats for seven passengers here.

Pegasus engine
The 910hp radial engine gave the Empire a range of 1,200km.

Variable-pitch propeller
The blades changed angle to vary engine thrust.

Rear hold
Contained mail, freight and passengers' luggage.

Galley
Food was prepared on board by a steward. Lunch might comprise soup, hot or cold meat and vegetables, dessert and cheese.

The Empire flying boat was 27m long, with a wingspan of 35m. It had a maximum speed of 320kph and a range of 1,200km.

IN THE COCKPIT

The 18-tonne aircraft was flown by a crew of two – the pilot and first officer. They sat side by side in a cockpit equipped with dual controls so that either of them could fly it if necessary. They followed the normal aviation seating convention. The pilot sat in the left seat, the first officer in the right. The radio officer sat in a compartment behind them.

Upper deck windows

Radio aerial

Mast-head light

Retractable direction-finding aerial

Cockpit

Mooring compartment

Wing-tip float

Hull

MOORING

After landing, the plane was tied to a buoy. If no buoy was available, it dropped anchor. A compartment in front of the cockpit contained the necessary ropes and anchors.

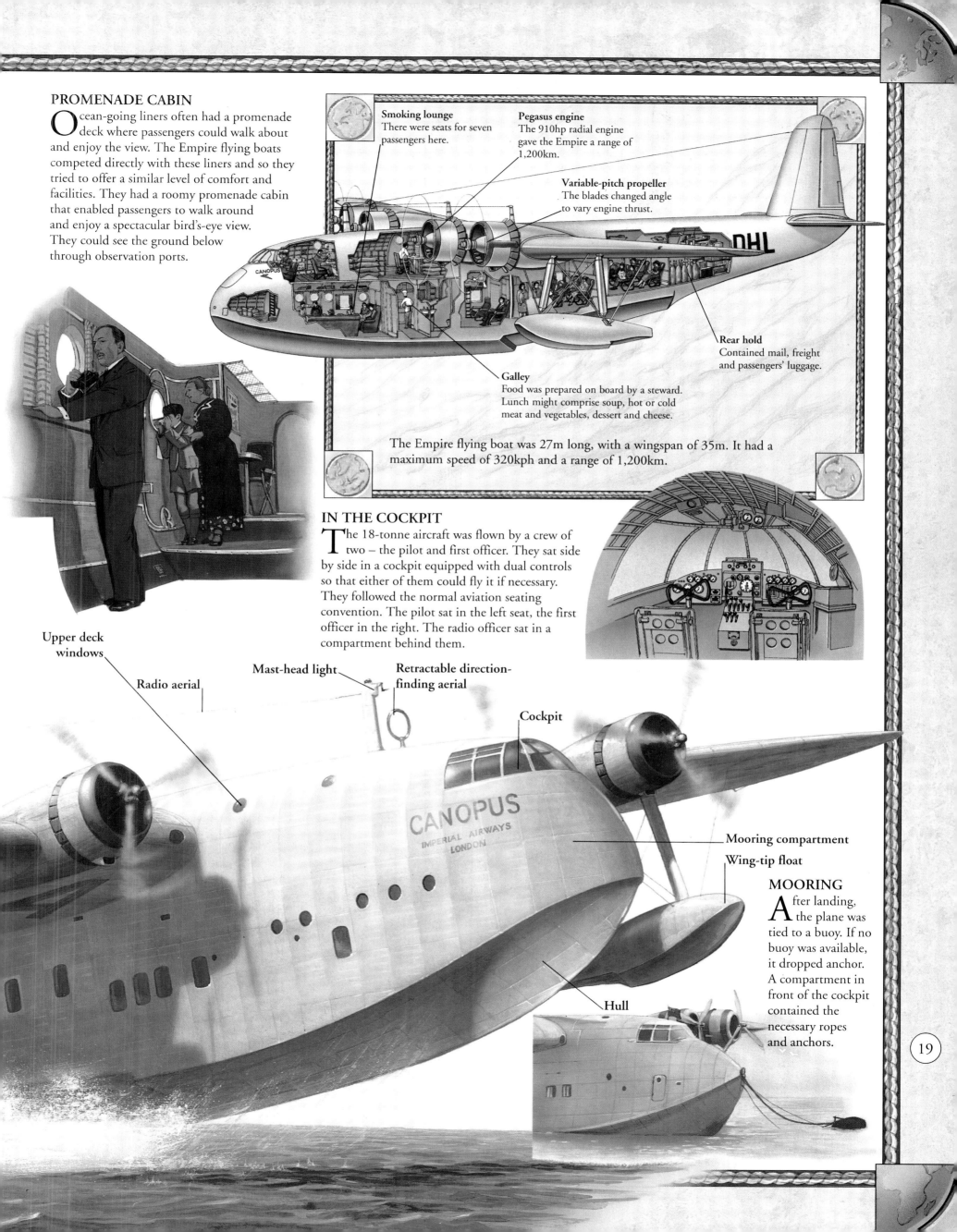

Timeless transporter

"Certainly the most famous airliner in aviation history, large numbers remain in civil and military service ..."
Michael Taylor and David Mondey
Guinness Book of Aircraft, Facts and Feats 1970

FLIGHT ATTENDANT

When the DC-3 came into service, uniformed flight attendants, or stewardesses as they were known then, were still a new part of air travel. They replaced the uniformed chefs and waiters that were carried on earlier aircraft. The stewardess shown above is wearing a nurse's uniform to show that she has proper nursing qualifications.

The Douglas DC-3 is the most successful commercial airliner ever built. Since the first one came into service in 1936, more than 13,000 have been produced, and some are still flying today. Each aircraft could carry up to 32 passengers, depending on the seating layout. Although the DC-3 had an unladen weight of 8,030 kilograms, it could travel at up to 318 kilometres per hour. The DC-3 entered airline service in 1936 as a sleeper aircraft. It was so successful that by 1939, 90 per cent of the world's airline passengers were carried in DC-3s. They were flown by a crew of two, with a stewardess to look after the passengers. Although the DC-3 was built originally as a civilian aircraft, most DC-3s were military versions built during World War 2 (1939-1945). After the war, these were bought up by airlines. One type of DC-3, the C-47, was called the "Dakota". Since then, all versions of the DC-3 have been known as Dakotas.

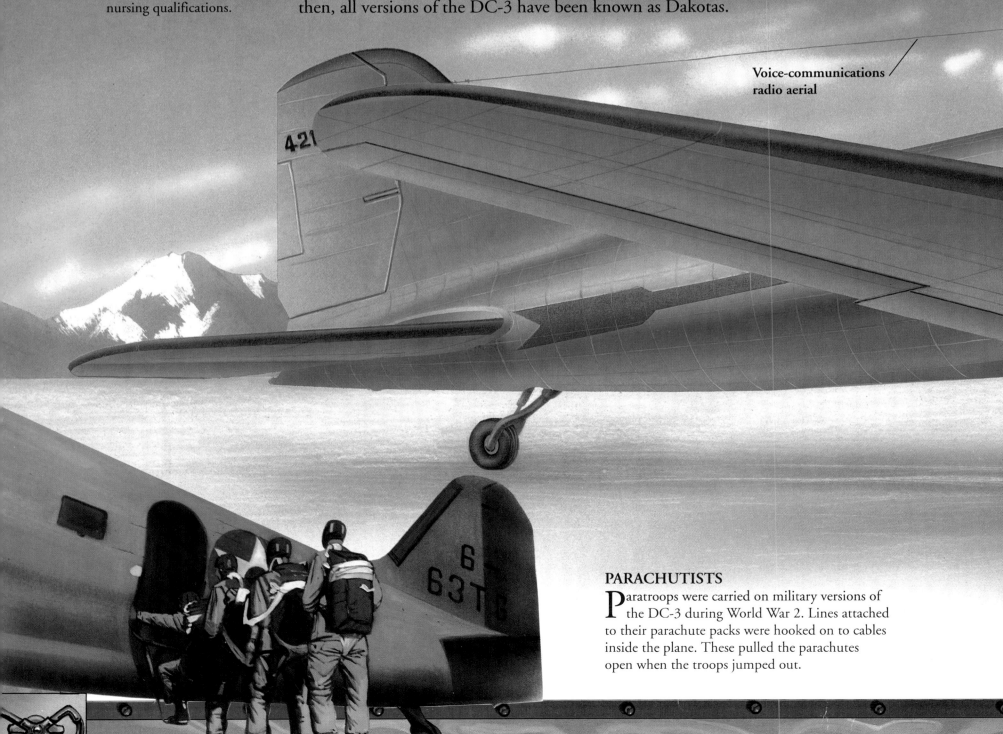

Voice-communications radio aerial

PARACHUTISTS

Paratroops were carried on military versions of the DC-3 during World War 2. Lines attached to their parachute packs were hooked on to cables inside the plane. These pulled the parachutes open when the troops jumped out.

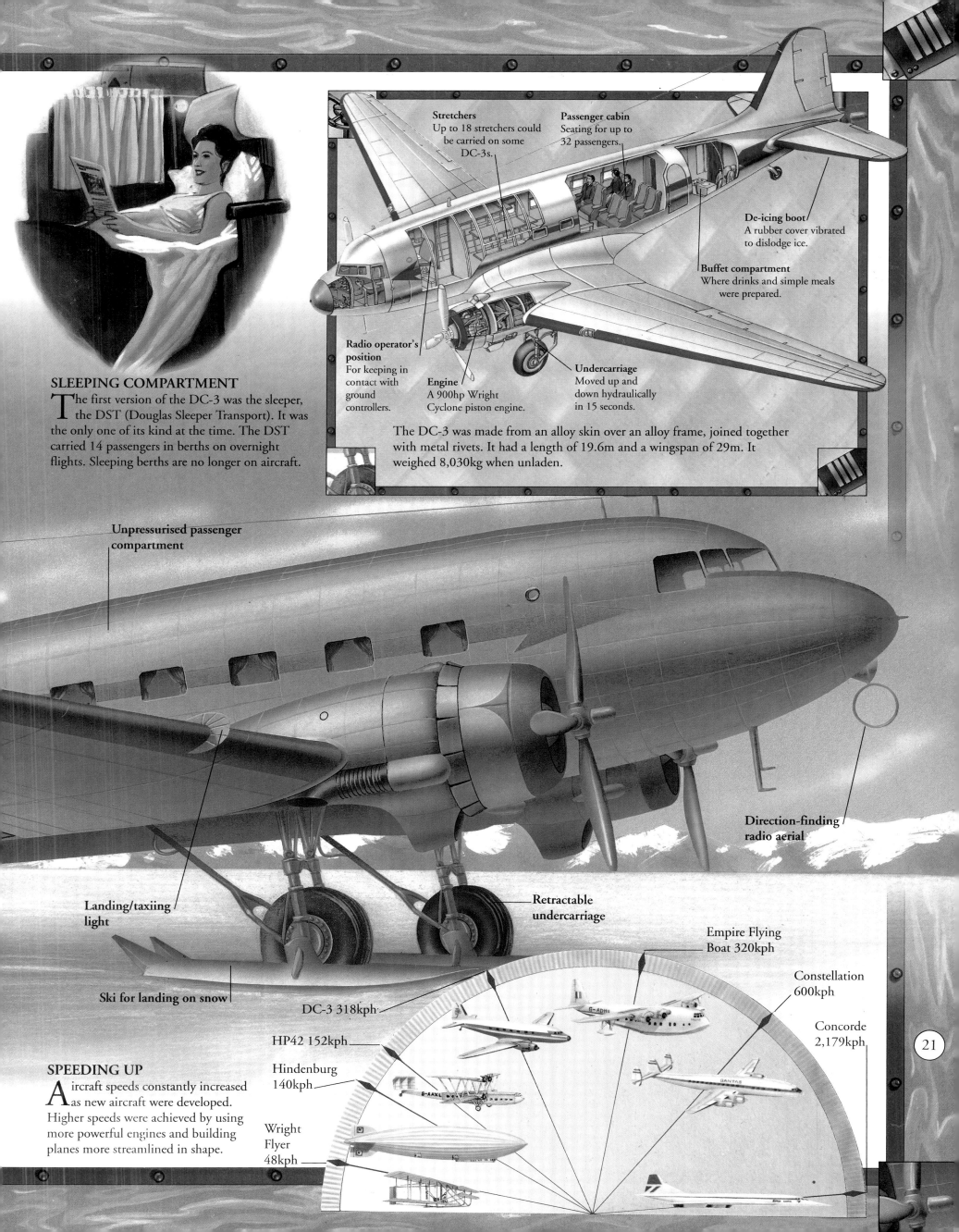

SLEEPING COMPARTMENT

The first version of the DC-3 was the sleeper, the DST (Douglas Sleeper Transport). It was the only one of its kind at the time. The DST carried 14 passengers in berths on overnight flights. Sleeping berths are no longer on aircraft.

Stretchers
Up to 18 stretchers could be carried on some DC-3s.

Passenger cabin
Seating for up to 32 passengers.

De-icing boot
A rubber cover vibrated to dislodge ice.

Buffet compartment
Where drinks and simple meals were prepared.

Radio operator's position
For keeping in contact with ground controllers.

Engine
A 900hp Wright Cyclone piston engine.

Undercarriage
Moved up and down hydraulically in 15 seconds.

The DC-3 was made from an alloy skin over an alloy frame, joined together with metal rivets. It had a length of 19.6m and a wingspan of 29m. It weighed 8,030kg when unladen.

Unpressurised passenger compartment

Direction-finding radio aerial

Landing/taxiing light

Retractable undercarriage

Ski for landing on snow

SPEEDING UP

Aircraft speeds constantly increased as new aircraft were developed. Higher speeds were achieved by using more powerful engines and building planes more streamlined in shape.

Empire Flying Boat 320kph

Constellation 600kph

Concorde 2,179kph

DC-3 318kph

HP42 152kph

Hindenburg 140kph

Wright Flyer 48kph

21

A fearsome fighter

"The fastest aircraft to fly before World War 2 was a special development of the German Messerschmitt Bf109 ... setting a record that was not beaten by another piston-engined aeroplane until 30 years later."
Michael Taylor and David Mondey *Guinness Book of Aircraft, Facts and Feats* 1970

The German Messerschmitt Bf109 was developed in the 1930s by Willy Messerschmitt. It became one of the fastest, most manoeuvrable and well-armed fighters of World War 2. Approximately 35,000 were built – more than any other fighter. It had a special system for supplying fuel to the engine, enabling it to perform manoeuvres which were impossible for other aircraft. The fastest version of the Bf109 could fly at up to 640 kilometres per hour and could reach a maximum height of 11,000 metres. It was a very popular aircraft with German pilots. They flew it high and fast, ready to accelerate to combat-speed and pounce on enemy fighters, or sweep down to attack slow-flying bombers. The Bf109's main fault was that it could not carry much fuel. It could only fly 660 kilometres without refuelling. With such a short range, the plane was not able to linger for very long in the important combat zone over southern England.

GROUND WAR ROOM

The routes of German bombers and their fighter escorts, which protected them, were plotted on a map in the huge Berlin war room. The commanders then knew exactly how many aircraft were in action, and their positions. Many escorts were made up of Bf109s. German bomber crews believed that the Bf109s protected them more effectively than any other fighter aircraft.

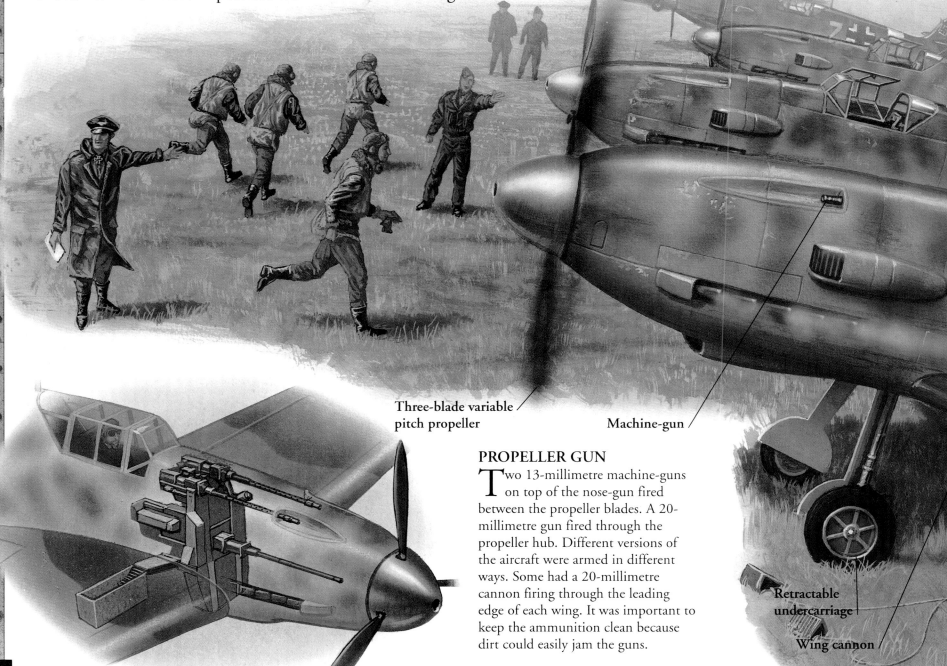

Three-blade variable pitch propeller

Machine-gun

PROPELLER GUN

Two 13-millimetre machine-guns on top of the nose-gun fired between the propeller blades. A 20-millimetre gun fired through the propeller hub. Different versions of the aircraft were armed in different ways. Some had a 20-millimetre cannon firing through the leading edge of each wing. It was important to keep the ammunition clean because dirt could easily jam the guns.

Retractable undercarriage

Wing cannon

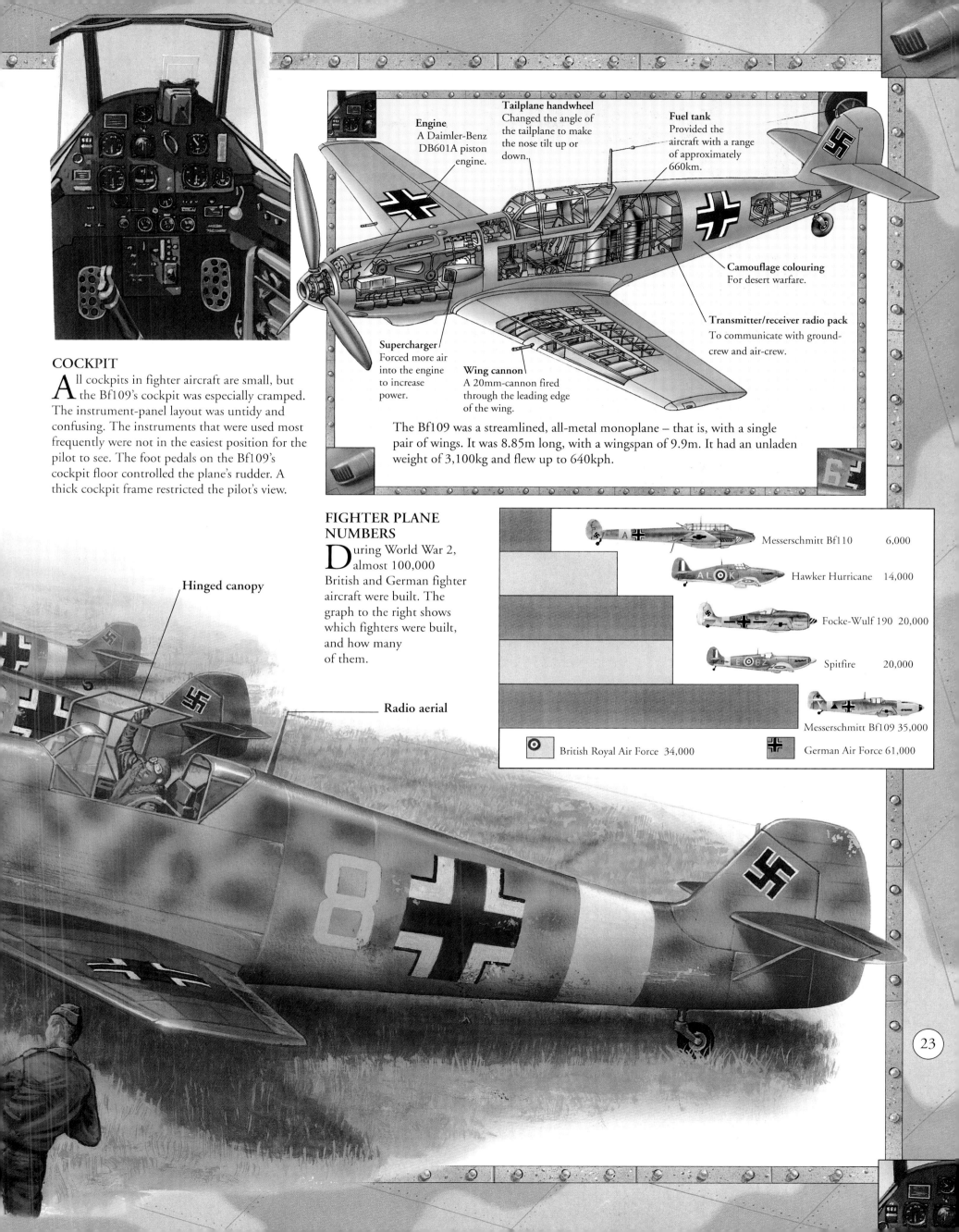

Engine
A Daimler-Benz
DB601A piston
engine.

Tailplane handwheel
Changed the angle of
the tailplane to make
the nose tilt up or
down.

Fuel tank
Provided the
aircraft with a range
of approximately
660km.

Camouflage colouring
For desert warfare.

Transmitter/receiver radio pack
To communicate with ground-
crew and air-crew.

Supercharger
Forced more air
into the engine
to increase
power.

Wing cannon
A 20mm-cannon fired
through the leading edge
of the wing.

The Bf109 was a streamlined, all-metal monoplane – that is, with a single
pair of wings. It was 8.85m long, with a wingspan of 9.9m. It had an unladen
weight of 3,100kg and flew up to 640kph.

COCKPIT

All cockpits in fighter aircraft are small, but
the Bf109's cockpit was especially cramped.
The instrument-panel layout was untidy and
confusing. The instruments that were used most
frequently were not in the easiest position for the
pilot to see. The foot pedals on the Bf109's
cockpit floor controlled the plane's rudder. A
thick cockpit frame restricted the pilot's view.

Hinged canopy

Radio aerial

FIGHTER PLANE NUMBERS

During World War 2,
almost 100,000
British and German fighter
aircraft were built. The
graph to the right shows
which fighters were built,
and how many
of them.

Messerschmitt Bf110   6,000

Hawker Hurricane   14,000

Focke-Wulf 190 20,000

Spitfire   20,000

Messerschmitt Bf109 35,000

British Royal Air Force 34,000   German Air Force 61,000

Bombs away

"The Lancaster was a thorough-bred. It looked magnificent on the ground – strong and well-proportioned. And it was powerful and well-balanced in the air. The ground-crews worked their hearts out to keep us flying. The riggers and fitters, the electricians, mechanics and armourers, they all took a pride in their aircraft."
Norman Mitchell, a Lancaster bomb aimer

MISSION MARKERS

Bomber crews kept a tally of the number of missions they flew by painting a bomb on the aircraft's nose for each mission, which was called a sortie. This Lancaster has flown 47 sorties. Some flew more than 100. Most missions took place at night, when enemy fighter planes could not operate so successfully.

EMBLEMS

Each bomber crew tried to make its aircraft a little different from all the others. They gave the aircraft a name and painted a colourful emblem on its nose. This one shows a lion (a symbol of Britain) eating a German flag.

The British Avro Lancaster was one of the most successful heavy bombers of World War 2. More than 7,300 were built. It flew 156,318 bombing missions, and dropped a total of 618,000 tonnes of bombs. It could carry a heavier bomb, and at a higher altitude, than any similar aircraft and was very manoeuvrable for its large size. Flying a Lancaster was a physically demanding job. The crew flew to an altitude of 6,700 metres for up to 12 hours. This meant that they had to breathe oxygen through a face mask often in temperatures as low as -5°C. The Lancasters rarely had fighter escorts, and flew mostly at night to avoid being attacked.

Mid-upper gun turret

Rear-gun turret

Twin-fin tail

BOMB LOADING

Heavy bombs were driven to a Lancaster on a train of trailers pulled by a tractor. The bombs were then lifted up on to racks inside the bomb bay. The ten-metre long bomb bay could carry different bomb loads. When loaded, the plane took a long time to take off because of the heavy weight.

BOMB STATISTICS

As the war progressed, larger bombs were produced. The doors of the bomb bay were therefore adapted so that they curved outwards to carry the bombs.

450kg

1,320kg "Bouncing bomb"

3,640kg "Blockbuster"

5,450kg "Tallboy"

10,000kg "Grand Slam"

FLIGHT PLANS AND LOG BOOKS

About three hours before a mission, the crew attended a briefing where they were told what their target for that night was to be. The outward and return routes were plotted on a map, or flight plan. Pilots kept a careful record of all their missions in a log book.

Engine
One of four 1,460hp Rolls-Royce Merlin piston engines.

Tail-guns
Four machine-guns protected the aircraft's tail.

Ammunition boxes
Supplied ammunition to the gun turrets.

Fuel tanks
These enabled the plane to fly 2,784km with a bomb load of 5,443kg, and 4,072km with a bomb load of 3,175kg.

Machine-guns
Two 7.7-mm machine-guns in nose turret.

Bomb aimer's position
Bomb aimer also fired the front gun.

Dark underside camouflage
Helped conceal the plane from the ground on night-flying missions.

The Lancaster had a length of 21.2m, a wingspan of 31.1m, and a maximum take-off weight of 32,659kg. Its powerful Rolls-Royce Merlin engines gave it a maximum speed of 460kph at a height of 6,700m. The huge bomb bay could carry a load of up to 10,000kg.

Camouflage colours

Front-gun turret

Bomb aimer's window

Bomb bay (open)

LANCASTER CREW

The Lancaster had a crew of seven. They wore up to seven layers of clothing to keep warm during the flight.

1. Wireless operator   2. Front gunner/bomb aimer   3. Flight engineer   4. Navigator   5. Pilot   6. Central gunner   7. Rear gunner

Queen of the airways

"The Constellations have more new features than any other airliner in a decade. They add up to greater speed, a higher degree of safety, more comfort and bigger and better menus."
Norman Ellison *Sydney Sun* 1947

The Lockheed Constellation was first developed in 1938 as a commercial airliner, but the planes were taken over by the United States Army during World War 2. After the war, the Constellation was developed as a long-haul airliner for commercial flights. It was the first of the post-war airliners and was extensively developed to make long flights more attractive with its extra passenger comfort. Over the years there were many improvements on the first type of Constellation, although its drooping nose and upswept tail remained the same. Super Constellations developed, which had a fuselage that was longer, but a wingspan that remained the same. After this, came "Starliners". These had a fuselage and wings that were longer than those of the Super Constellation. Inside the aircraft, each version of the Constellation introduced new standards in passenger service. A comfortable reclining sleeper seat was first used in an Air Ceylon Constellation in 1956. The elegant Constellation was used until the late 1970s. The aircraft shown on the right is the 1049G, which was a Super Constellation. There were 26 versions of the Constellation and 49 versions of the Super Constellation.

TRANSCONTINENTAL ROUTES

The Constellation helped to open the post-war long-range air routes. Transcontinental services began in 1946 with flights between New York and Bournemouth, and London and Rio de Janeiro.

Triple-fin tail

Upswept tail

De-icing strip

Wing-tip fuel tank

RADAR

In the 1950s the first Super Constellations used in the United States Air Force were transferred from the navy and refitted with a rotating radar dish called a rotodome, shown above. Airborne radar detects enemy planes further away than radar on the ground.

LANDING GEAR

Almost all airliners before the Constellation had a main wheel under each wing and one under the tail. The Constellation had a "tricycle" undercarriage; the wheels were arranged with one at the front and one under each wing, so the passenger cabin was parallel to the ground.

COCKTAIL LOUNGE

Lockheed spent 1,500,000 US dollars and 120,000 working hours giving the Super Constellation the most luxurious interior of any large passenger aircraft. The cocktail lounge had special lighting effects and peaceful colour schemes to make it more relaxing.

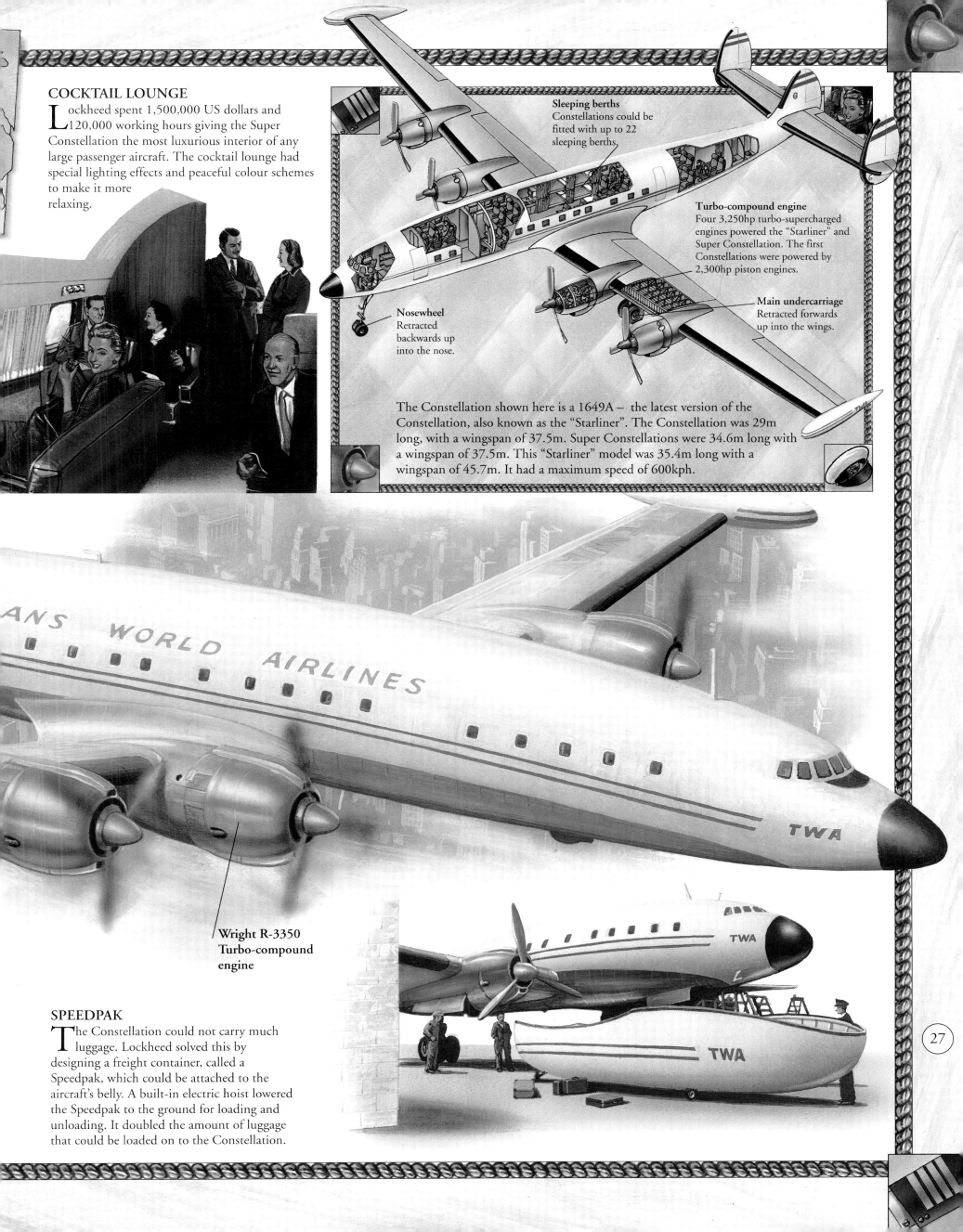

Sleeping berths
Constellations could be fitted with up to 22 sleeping berths.

Turbo-compound engine
Four 3,250hp turbo-supercharged engines powered the "Starliner" and Super Constellation. The first Constellations were powered by 2,300hp piston engines.

Nosewheel
Retracted backwards up into the nose.

Main undercarriage
Retracted forwards up into the wings.

The Constellation shown here is a 1649A — the latest version of the Constellation, also known as the "Starliner". The Constellation was 29m long, with a wingspan of 37.5m. Super Constellations were 34.6m long with a wingspan of 37.5m. This "Starliner" model was 35.4m long with a wingspan of 45.7m. It had a maximum speed of 600kph.

Wright R-3350 Turbo-compound engine

SPEEDPAK

The Constellation could not carry much luggage. Lockheed solved this by designing a freight container, called a Speedpak, which could be attached to the aircraft's belly. A built-in electric hoist lowered the Speedpak to the ground for loading and unloading. It doubled the amount of luggage that could be loaded on to the Constellation.

Higher and faster

"The Comet was years ahead of the competition, pioneering jet transportation high above the weather, and achieving journey times half that expected with piston-engined aircraft."
Philip J Birtles *Classic Civil Aircraft 3: de Havilland Comet* 1993

Research into faster military aircraft during World War 2 speeded up the development of jet engines. At the end of the war, work began on developing jet airliners. The first jet airliner to enter service was the British de Havilland Comet 1 in 1952. It was popular with passengers because it was able to fly higher and faster than any piston-engined airliner. Shorter flights to faraway places, higher above stormy weather, were less tiring and stressful for the passengers. Comets could reach Singapore in 25 hours, or Tokyo in 36 hours. These journeys would have taken almost twice as long in a Super Constellation! But the Comet 1 had its problems, from which all aircraft manufacturers learned. The aircraft was grounded in 1954 after a series of crashes. Investigators found that the greater difference in air pressure between the inside and outside of the high-flying aeroplane put extra stress on the fuselage, which eventually cracked open in flight. The aircraft was strengthened and enlarged as the Comet 4, shown here, which entered service in 1958.

STRESS ANALYSIS

Following three crashes of the Comet, scientists searched for any fault that might have caused the accidents. The scientists had a Comet sealed inside a pressurised water tank to simulate the stresses of flight. In tests, the fuselage cracked open. The Comet's fuselage was strengthened and the problem ended.

Radio aerial (inside top of tail fin)

Pressurised passenger cabin

Rudder

Instrument Landing System aerial (inside tips of tail plane)

G-ALYT

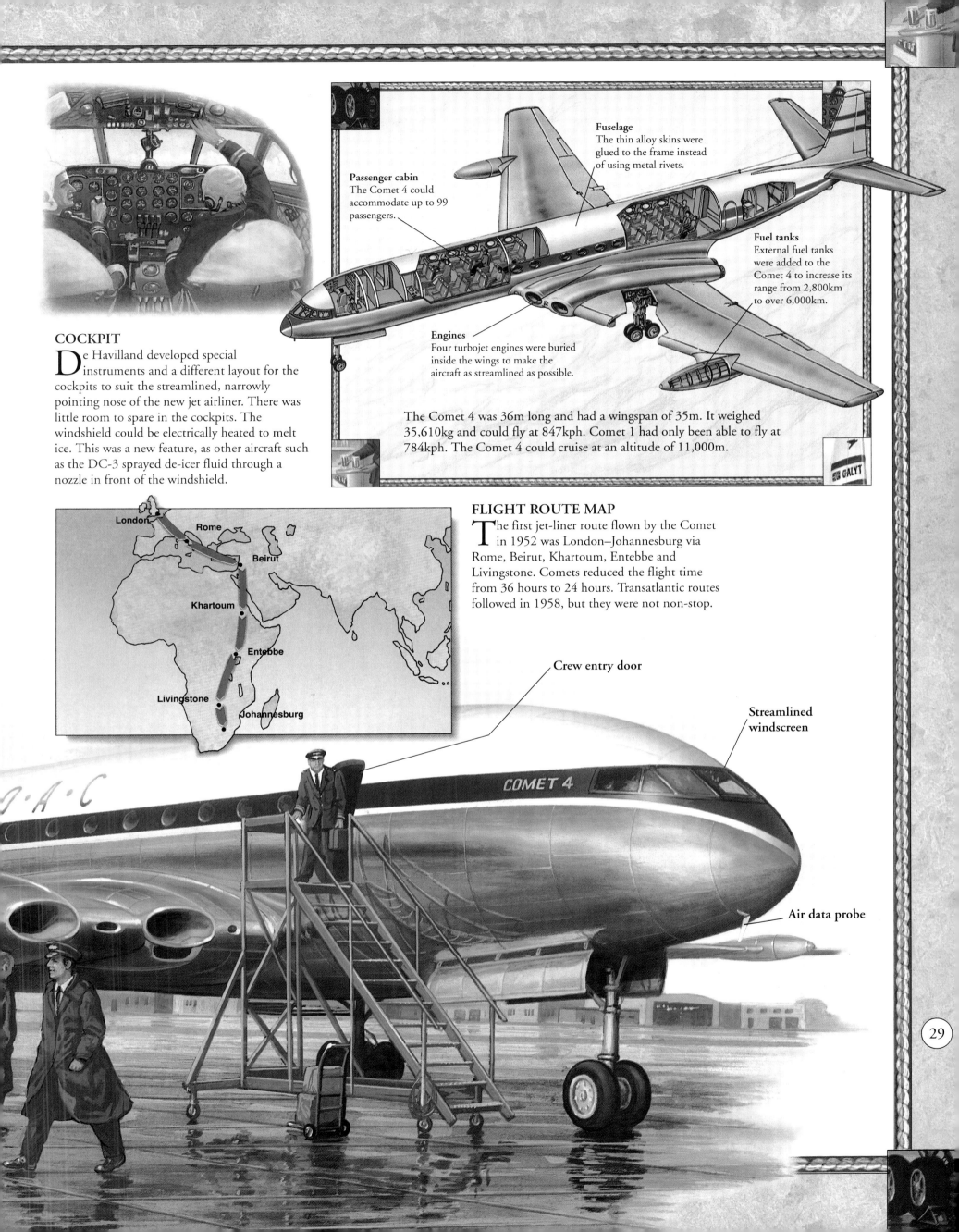

Passenger cabin
The Comet 4 could
accommodate up to 99
passengers.

Fuselage
The thin alloy skins were
glued to the frame instead
of using metal rivets.

Fuel tanks
External fuel tanks
were added to the
Comet 4 to increase its
range from 2,800km
to over 6,000km.

Engines
Four turbojet engines were buried
inside the wings to make the
aircraft as streamlined as possible.

The Comet 4 was 36m long and had a wingspan of 35m. It weighed
35,610kg and could fly at 847kph. Comet 1 had only been able to fly at
784kph. The Comet 4 could cruise at an altitude of 11,000m.

COCKPIT

De Havilland developed special
instruments and a different layout for the
cockpits to suit the streamlined, narrowly
pointing nose of the new jet airliner. There was
little room to spare in the cockpits. The
windshield could be electrically heated to melt
ice. This was a new feature, as other aircraft such
as the DC-3 sprayed de-icer fluid through a
nozzle in front of the windshield.

FLIGHT ROUTE MAP

The first jet-liner route flown by the Comet
in 1952 was London–Johannesburg via
Rome, Beirut, Khartoum, Entebbe and
Livingstone. Comets reduced the flight time
from 36 hours to 24 hours. Transatlantic routes
followed in 1958, but they were not non-stop.

London
Rome
Beirut
Khartoum
Entebbe
Livingstone
Johannesburg

Crew entry door

**Streamlined
windscreen**

COMET 4

Air data probe

Mighty monster

"Loading and pre-flight checks took 45 minutes. We normally took a ten-minute break before engine start to get the sweat out of our suits or we'd freeze at altitude."
Captain Don Jansky, B-52 pilot

The American B-52 Stratofortress was first designed in the mid-1940s as a heavy bomber. It developed in the 1950s as a long-range nuclear bomber because World War 2 had shown that the long-range heavy bomber was the most threatening weapon available to attack an enemy's territory. The huge aircraft is known affectionately by its crews as the "Buff", the Big Ugly Fat Fella. It has never dropped a nuclear bomb, but it has been used for non-nuclear bombing.

Its crew enters the aircraft through a small hatch in its belly. The aircraft commander and co-pilot fly the plane from their side-by-side seats in the cockpit. Behind them, facing backwards, sits the defensive team of electronic warfare officers. One of them also operates the tail-gun.

Early B-52 crews wore an uncomfortable skin-tight pressure suit. It inflated automatically if the cabin pressure was lost. Later, B-52s were flown at much lower altitudes to avoid detection by enemy radar. Pressure suits then became unnecessary.

The "Buff" has lasted a long time because it has been updated regularly. Different versions of the latest model of the B-52 exist, including reconnaissance versions. The B-52 can hold many different combinations of weapons. It is the world's heaviest bomber, and can carry up to 45,000kg of bombs.

TAIL-GUN

The B-52's only defensive armament has been in its tail. The model shown here has a six-barrelled machine-gun. Early models were armed with four machine-guns.

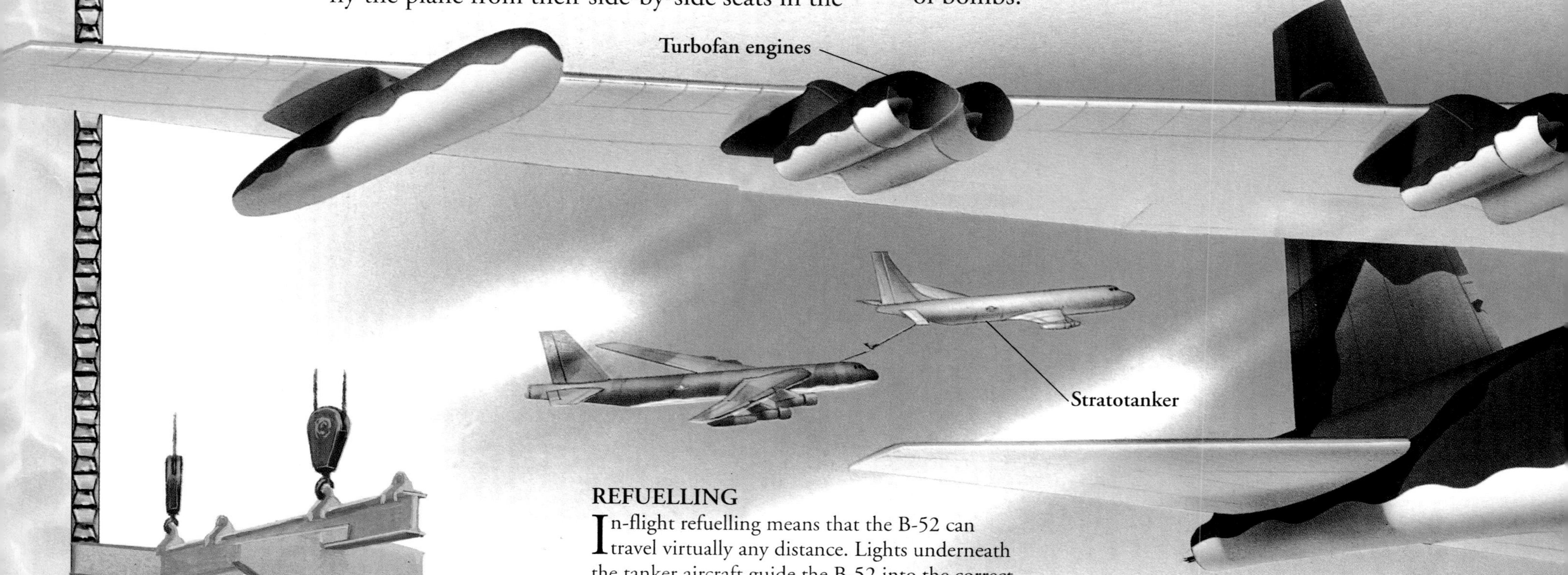

Turbofan engines

Stratotanker

REFUELLING

In-flight refuelling means that the B-52 can travel virtually any distance. Lights underneath the tanker aircraft guide the B-52 into the correct position for refuelling.

ENGINE

All B-52 Stratofortresses except for the latest model, the B-52H, were powered by eight turbojets, grouped in four pairs. The B-52H is powered by eight turbofans, like the one shown here, because these are quieter and use less fuel than turbojets. They also increase power performance dramatically, allowing the aircraft to take off quickly. These engines can run for 4,000 hours before needing a service – the older turbojets could run for only 500 hours between services.

TAKING OFF

The chart below compares the maximum take-off weight of the B-52 with that of other aircraft in this book.

B-52H Stratofortress	221,353kg
Avro Lancaster B-1	32,659kg
Lockheed F-117A	23,814kg
Sopwith Camel	672kg

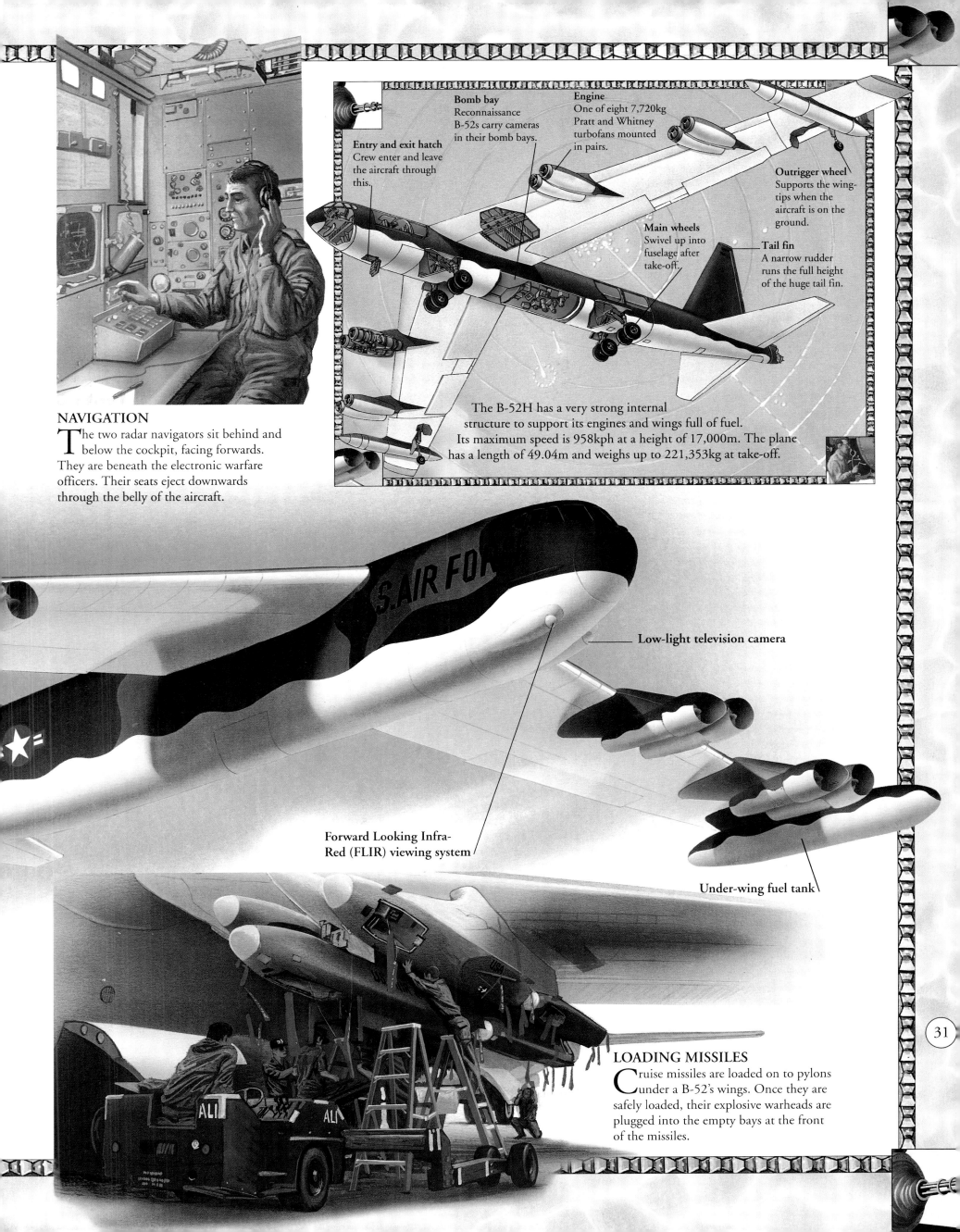

NAVIGATION

The two radar navigators sit behind and below the cockpit, facing forwards. They are beneath the electronic warfare officers. Their seats eject downwards through the belly of the aircraft.

Bomb bay
Reconnaissance B-52s carry cameras in their bomb bays.

Engine
One of eight 7,720kg Pratt and Whitney turbofans mounted in pairs.

Entry and exit hatch
Crew enter and leave the aircraft through this.

Outrigger wheel
Supports the wing-tips when the aircraft is on the ground.

Main wheels
Swivel up into fuselage after take-off.

Tail fin
A narrow rudder runs the full height of the huge tail fin.

The B-52H has a very strong internal structure to support its engines and wings full of fuel. Its maximum speed is 958kph at a height of 17,000m. The plane has a length of 49.04m and weighs up to 221,353kg at take-off.

S. AIR FOR

Low-light television camera

Forward Looking Infra-Red (FLIR) viewing system

Under-wing fuel tank

LOADING MISSILES

Cruise missiles are loaded on to pylons under a B-52's wings. Once they are safely loaded, their explosive warheads are plugged into the empty bays at the front of the missiles.

Whirlybird

The first helicopters were not very strong and could not carry a heavy load, so they were not suited to military requirements. But in the 1950s, the Boeing-Vertol CH-47 Chinook answered the US Army's need for a very powerful helicopter. It had to be one that could transport at least 40 troops and carry a two-tonne load inside it. The helicopter also had to be able to fly with an eight-tonne load slung underneath it. The Chinook can do this and more. It has become a valuable multipurpose air-truck for transporting troops and equipment. Military forces all over the world use this helicopter. Two sets of controls allow either the pilot or co-pilot, sitting side by side, to fly the aircraft. The Chinook, like most modern helicopters, is powered by turboshaft jet engines. These are fitted at the rear of the aircraft and linked to the rotor blades by spinning shafts. Noise and vibration from the rotor blades are so great that the crew talk to each other through intercoms.

Rear rotor

US ARMY 981143

ARMY

Textron Lycoming T55-L-712 turboshaft engine

Radio aerial

Cargo ramp

Main cargo hook

LOADING RAMP

With the rear loading ramp lowered, vehicles can be driven straight into and out of the helicopter. The Chinook can move small vehicles quickly by air to wherever they are needed.

ROTOR BLADES

The Chinook's twin-rotor layout, with rotor blades at each end, enables it to fly with a longer, more spacious fuselage than other helicopters. It is more stable, so it can lift heavy equipment on hooks underneath the fuselage. The long blades overlap, but they are arranged so that they cannot hit each other. They rotate in opposite directions so that the spinning forces that they put on to the helicopter cancel each other out. The rotor blades are made from glass fibre. Extra-tough titanium is used on the leading edges of the blades.

Stick boost actuators
Provide extra power to operate the flying controls.

Transmission shaft
Transfers engine power to the front rotor.

Fuel tank
Holds 2,068 litres of fuel.

Engine-intake screen
Keeps dust and larger objects out of the engine.

Drive shaft
Links the engine to the rear rotor.

The Chinook is unusual because it has two overhead rotors, one at the front and the other at the rear. Fuel is stored in the bulge running down each side of the fuselage. The helicopter weighs 10,151kg unladen.

Front rotor

Air data probes

Emergency exit window

SKI SHOES

As a military aircraft, the Chinook has to be able to operate in all weather conditions. Its landing gear can be fitted with ski shoes for coming down on snow or ice. The broad surface of the ski shoes spreads the weight of the aircraft to stop it sinking into the ground.

TROOP LITTERS

The Chinook can be adapted for many uses. One of the Chinook's most important roles is evacuating casualties during wartime. It can be fitted with up to 22 litters (stretchers) stacked four deep, down each side of the fuselage.

TROOP SEATING

The Chinook is designed to carry 44 seated troops on a normal flight, although on one occasion, it carried 81 paratroopers! The bench-type seats are arranged down each side of the aircraft to save space, and are made from nylon sheet stretched over a tubular aluminium frame.

PASSENGER SEATING

A civilian version of the Chinook was used to transport passengers. For example, it would take oil workers to off-shore oil rigs. The bare military interior and seating were replaced by more comfortable airline-style seats. The Chinook is no longer used for civilian purposes.

Spyplane

"The windscreen gets so hot that a pilot can't keep his hand on it for more than 20 seconds even with flame-retardant gloves."
Captain Thomas L. Peterson, Blackbird pilot

The Lockheed SR-71 entered service in the 1960s as a high-altitude, ultra-fast spyplane. It is the world's first stealth aircraft, and holds the world air-speed record of 3,529 kilometres per hour. It flies at an altitude of 26,000 metres, higher than most other aircraft. But more than this, the SR-71 can avoid detection on enemy radar screens because of its black, radar-absorbent paint and its unique shape. Its colour has earned the SR-71 the name "Blackbird".

The preparations for each flight begin with two hours of pre-flight checks. While the air-crew, the pilot and a reconnaissance (spying) systems operator (RSO), put on their pressure suits, the ground-crew start up all the aircraft's systems – from electricity generators and computers to life-support systems. The crew climb into their cramped cockpit nearly an hour before take-off. At its maximum speed, its cameras can photograph 259,000 square kilometres of the ground every hour.

PRESSURE SUIT
Blackbirds fly at such great altitude that their pilots wear pressure suits and helmets similar to an astronaut's spacesuit. The suit completely seals the pilot inside. The suit has to be supplied with oxygen for the pilot to breathe.

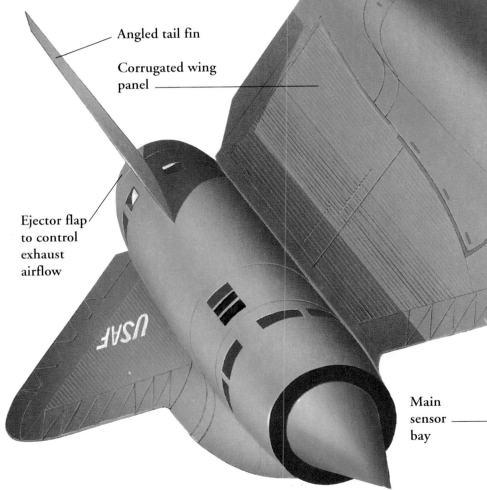

Angled tail fin

Corrugated wing panel

Ejector flap to control exhaust airflow

Main sensor bay

SPY PHOTOS
Despite the speed at which it flies, clear photographs can be taken from Blackbird on its spy missions by panoramic and long-range cameras held in the main sensor bay. The picture above was taken on a practice flight and shows the Los Angeles coastline in California, USA.

PARACHUTE
The Blackbird needs some help to stop from its touch-down speed of 278 kilometres per hour. A compartment in the top of the fuselage opens and a huge parachute streams out. The drag this creates slows the Blackbird to a halt within about 1,000 metres.

Fuel tanks
The total capacity of the fuel tanks is 46,182 litres.

Centre-body bleed louvres
Allow excess air to bleed out of the engine.

Skin
Made from titanium and covered with radar-absorbent paint.

Wheels
Contain nitrogen to keep them cool and prevent them from burning with the friction of landing.

Intake spike
Moves backwards and forwards to control engine air intake.

Engine
Pratt and Whitney J58 provides over 13,610kg thrust.

The Blackbird is made from titanium because this can withstand the high temperatures of mach 3.5 flight. The plane has a length of 33m and a wingspan of 17m. It weighs 27,216kg unladen.

Engine air intake

Delta wing

Flattened fuselage

SPEED COMPARISONS

The Blackbird flies faster than any other aircraft, and higher than any except for the Lockheed U-2, developed before the Blackbird, and the Russian MiG-25R.

1. Lockheed SR-71
   mach 3.5   3,529kph
2. Concorde
   mach 2.2   2,179kph
3. McDonnell Douglas Harrier
   1,040kph
4. Lockheed Constellation
   600kph
5. Douglas DC-3
   318kph
6. Wright Flyer
   48kph

Air data probes

In-flight refuelling receptacle

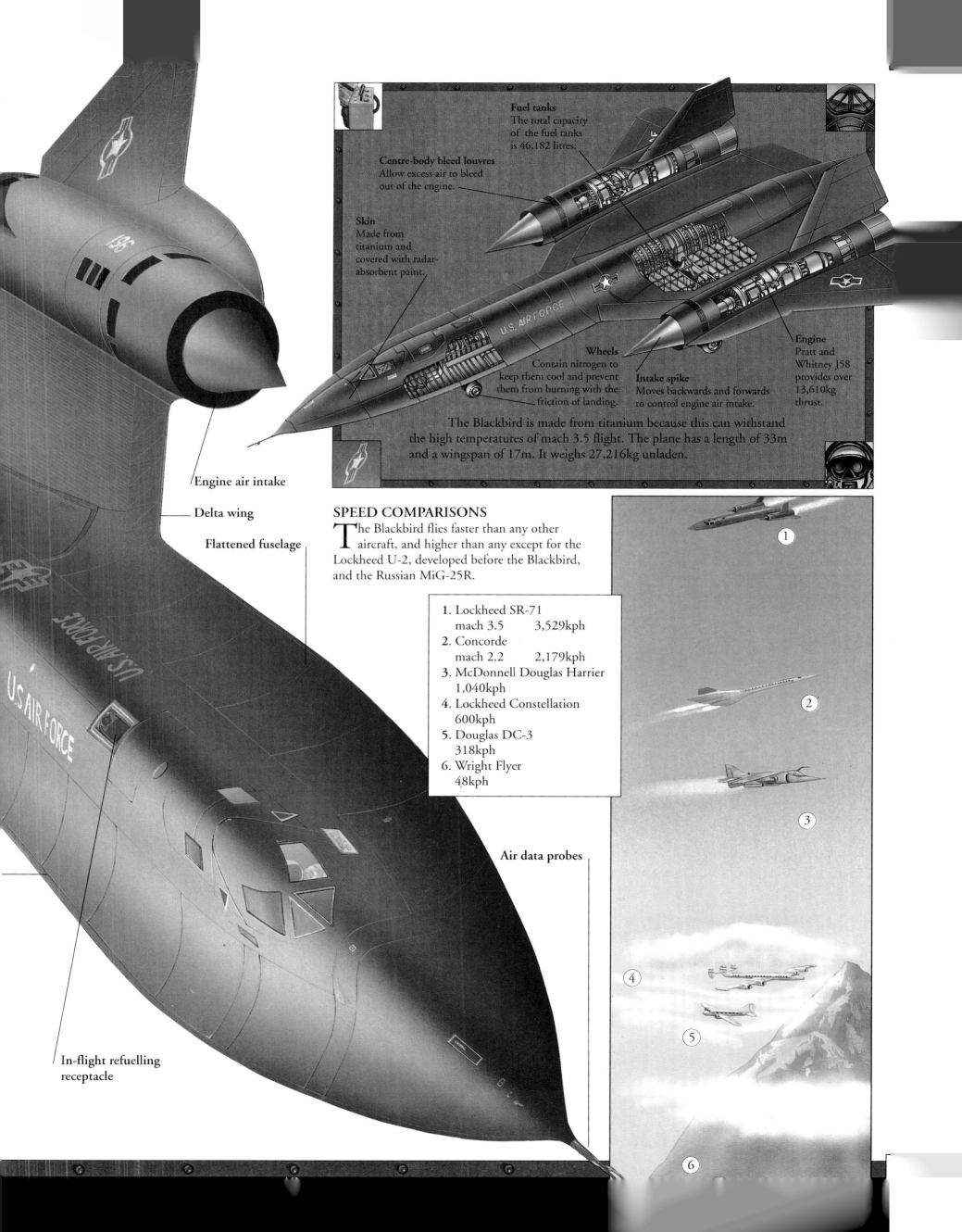

Hoverfly

"What's surprising ... for an aircraft with such extraordinary flying characteristics ... is it's very easy to fly."
Captain Charles "Chuck" Maloney, US Harrier pilot

This unusual military aircraft was developed during the 1960s and first flew in 1967. The Harrier is capable of flying in ways that are impossible for other aircraft. It can take off and land vertically like a helicopter, which has earned it the name "Jump Jet". This means that it can be used during warfare even if runways are destroyed. It can also hover motionless in the sky and even fly backwards! A single lever controls the position of the plane's engine nozzles, which gives this aircraft its special mobility. The nozzles are rotated to point downwards or backwards by moving the lever. Sitting on an ejector seat, the pilot commands this fast-attack aircraft from a cockpit with good all-round visibility. The Harrier can carry a selection of missiles and bombs. Two gun pods under the fuselage can each hold 100 shells.

FLYING GEAR

Harrier pilots wear a pressure suit with a life preserver, which inflates if they ditch in the sea. The suit also squeezes the pilot's legs when the Harrier makes sharp turns. This stops blood draining from the pilot's head.

VERTICAL TAKE-OFF

The arrows on the diagram above show the direction the plane is flying. Before the plane takes off, the engine nozzles point downwards. The pilot opens the throttle near his left thigh to increase the engine's thrust, and the plane rises vertically. The pilot then rotates the engine nozzles until they point backwards, and the blast of exhaust gases pushes the plane forwards.

Cooling air intake

Rocket pod

Tail radar

Air brake

MN 159246 MARINES

VMA231

05

SKI JUMP

The Harrier can carry more fuel and weapons if it takes off from a runway instead of vertically. This is because vertical take-off uses more power. The Harrier's take-off run can be shortened by sloping the end of the runway upwards. This is especially useful when Harriers have to operate from aircraft carriers. These ships have a sloped deck called a "ski jump". A Harrier with a heavy load can take to the air from this runway. On its return, and with a lighter load, the Harrier can land vertically. This is the safest way to land on a ship's deck.

ENGINE

The blast of exhaust gas is directed from the engine through four nozzles that can be rotated. This provides the thrust to power the Harrier.

Engine
This has about 9,760kg thrust.

Fuel tank
Located behind the engine.

Canopy
Gives pilot 360° visibility.

Engine nozzle
There are four of these geared together so they all point in the same direction.

Outrigger wheel
Helps to steady aircraft.

Wing-tip jet
Controls the plane's position when it hovers.

Rack
Racks under each wing carry bombs, missiles and fuel tanks.

The Harrier AV8-A has a maximum speed of 1,040kph. It is 14.12m long with a wingspan of 9.25m.

Auxiliary air intake

In-flight refuelling probe

Yaw vane

Cockpit air intake

Gun pod

CONTROL LEVERS

The nozzle lever controls the angle of the engine exhaust nozzles. The throttle increases the engine's thrust. The Short Take-Off Stop and Vertical Take-Off Stop mark the places for the nozzle lever to be positioned to take off from ski jumps (short take-off), or to take off vertically.

1. Throttle
2. Short Take-Off Stop
3. Nozzle lever
4. Vertical Take-Off Stop

INSTRUMENT PANEL

Screens display radar warning, navigation and engine data, as well as the weapons status and a map that shows the land beneath the Harrier as it is flying. The most important data, such as speed, altitude and any possible threat, is projected on a glass plate, or "head-up display", in the pilot's line of sight.

37

Faster than sound

"It's the closest thing to space travel I'm ever likely to experience, yet it seemed so normal. Concorde really is a remarkable aircraft. It gives you the opportunity to be a shirt-sleeve astronaut."
Peter Johnson, a Concorde passenger

Concorde is the world's first supersonic commercial passenger aircraft operating regular scheduled flights. Concorde was developed jointly by Britain and France during the 1960s and 1970s, when the DC-3, the Constellation and the Comet 4s were in regular service. No other aircraft can match Concorde's dreamlike performance and comfort. Nor can any other aircraft fly faster than sound over great distances without requiring in-flight refuelling. A few military aircraft can fly faster, but they need in-flight refuelling to fly as far. Concorde flies high through the atmosphere on the edge of space. At an altitude of 18 kilometres, flying at 2,179 kilometres per hour, passengers can see the curve of the Earth's surface. But there is no sensation of speed. The aircraft seems to hang motionless in the air, yet the lightning speed makes the windows feel warm because of friction with the air outside.

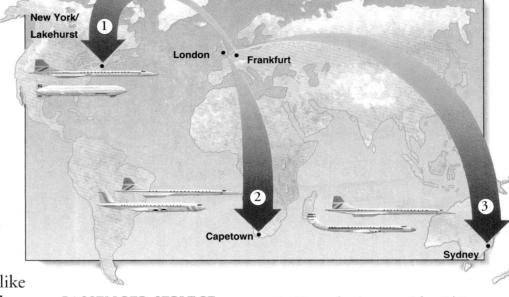

PASSENGER SERVICE

The above map shows how Concorde has improved flight times across the world. This ability to fly so quickly and in such style has made Concorde an important service for the business community.

1. Transatlantic route: 2 hrs 54.5 mins by Concorde, 65 hrs by *Hindenburg* airship.
2. South African route: 8 hrs 8 mins by Concorde, 24 hrs by de Havilland Comet.
3. Australian route: 17 hrs 13mins by Concorde, 55 hrs 7 mins by Lockheed Constellation.

DROOP-SNOOT

Concorde's nose was designed to "droop", to give a clear view ahead for take-off and landing (1). The nose is raised for normal flight (2).

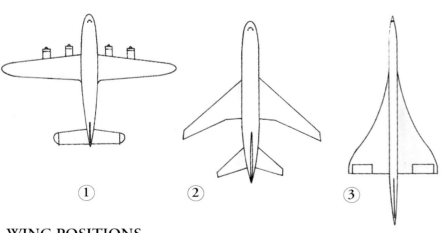

WING POSITIONS

The faster a plane is designed to fly, the more its wings have to be swept back. A piston-engined plane has straight wings (1). A jet airliner's wings are angled at 25-40 degrees (2). Concorde's wings are swept back so much that they form a triangular "delta" shape (3).

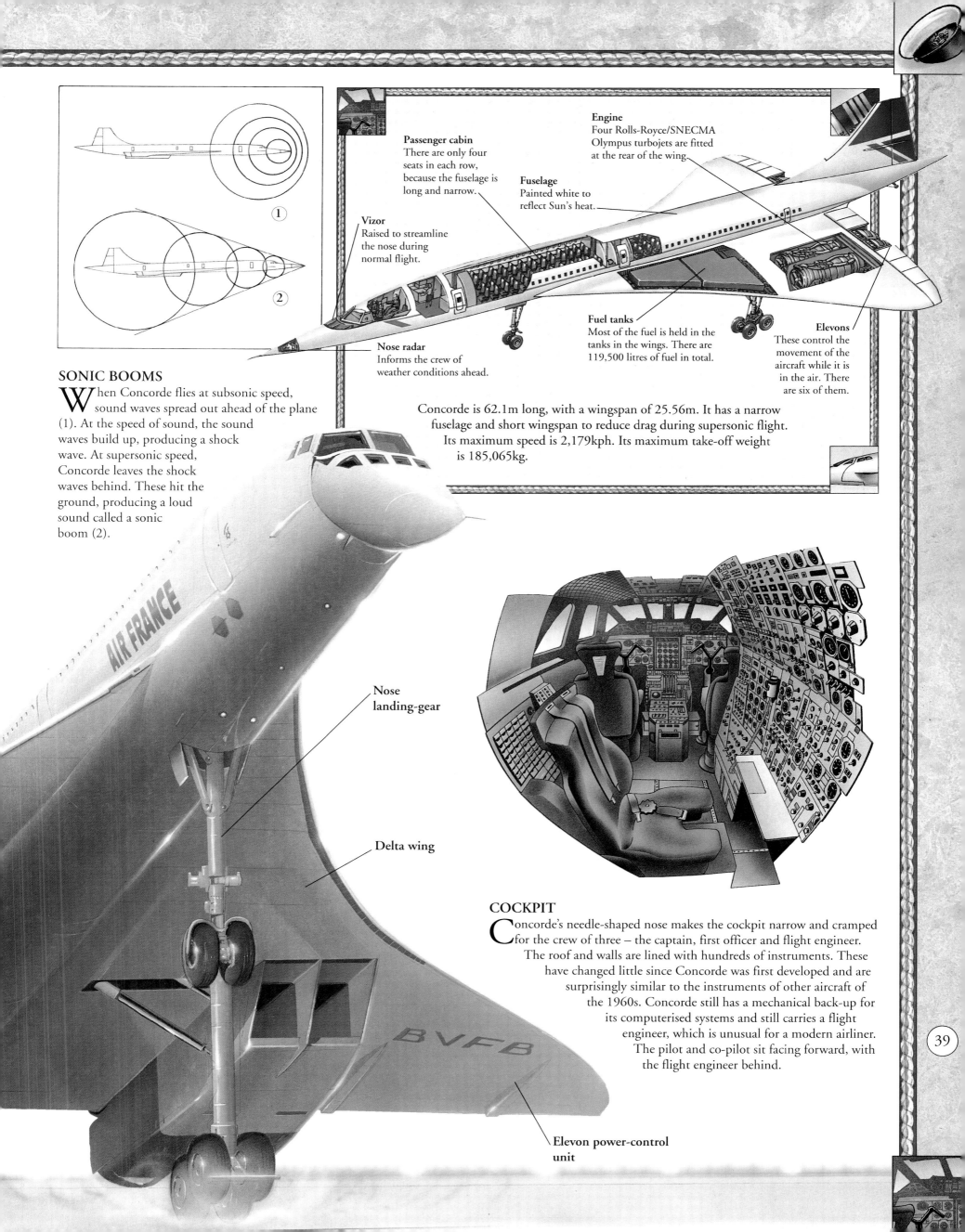

Passenger cabin
There are only four seats in each row, because the fuselage is long and narrow.

Engine
Four Rolls-Royce/SNECMA Olympus turbojets are fitted at the rear of the wing.

Fuselage
Painted white to reflect Sun's heat.

Vizor
Raised to streamline the nose during normal flight.

Nose radar
Informs the crew of weather conditions ahead.

Fuel tanks
Most of the fuel is held in the tanks in the wings. There are 119,500 litres of fuel in total.

Elevons
These control the movement of the aircraft while it is in the air. There are six of them.

Concorde is 62.1m long, with a wingspan of 25.56m. It has a narrow fuselage and short wingspan to reduce drag during supersonic flight. Its maximum speed is 2,179kph. Its maximum take-off weight is 185,065kg.

SONIC BOOMS

When Concorde flies at subsonic speed, sound waves spread out ahead of the plane (1). At the speed of sound, the sound waves build up, producing a shock wave. At supersonic speed, Concorde leaves the shock waves behind. These hit the ground, producing a loud sound called a sonic boom (2).

Nose landing-gear

Delta wing

Elevon power-control unit

COCKPIT

Concorde's needle-shaped nose makes the cockpit narrow and cramped for the crew of three – the captain, first officer and flight engineer. The roof and walls are lined with hundreds of instruments. These have changed little since Concorde was first developed and are surprisingly similar to the instruments of other aircraft of the 1960s. Concorde still has a mechanical back-up for its computerised systems and still carries a flight engineer, which is unusual for a modern airliner. The pilot and co-pilot sit facing forward, with the flight engineer behind.

The nighthawk

The Lockheed F-117A was designed to avoid detection by radar and also to mount precision attacks on its target. It is the world's first stealth combat aircraft. It is so difficult to detect either visually or by radar that it has earned the name "Nighthawk". The F-117A first flew in 1981 and first entered combat in 1989. It was designed not only to avoid detection by radar but also to mount precision attacks on its targets. The aircraft's pyramid shape is made up of many angled surfaces to reflect radar signals away from their source. It is made from a metal that is coated with a special material that also absorbs some of the radar signals that strike it. Once in the air, Nighthawk's computers fly it to within sight of the target so that the pilot can concentrate on delivering the weapons, which include air-to-air missiles and laser-guided bombs. Stealth fighters attack the most important and most heavily defended targets.

"We simply could not have done what we've done as effectively and efficiently, and at as low a cost to life, both our's and the enemy's, if we hadn't that stealth capability."
US Secretary of Defence, Dick Cheney, 1991

Butterfly tail fins

Flattened engine exhaust nozzle

Swept-back wing

SECURITY PALM PRINTS

Stealth fighters are protected by 24-hour security. Armed guards surround their hangars. An electronic security system checks authorised personnels' palm prints before they are allowed near the aircraft.

PAYLOAD

Stealth fighters are loaded with up to 2,268 kilograms of weapons. The choice of weaponry available includes laser-guided bombs, air-to-air missiles and air-to-surface missiles. Two bombs or missiles are carried side by side on racks in the central weapons bay. Two different types of weapons can be carried at the same time.

40

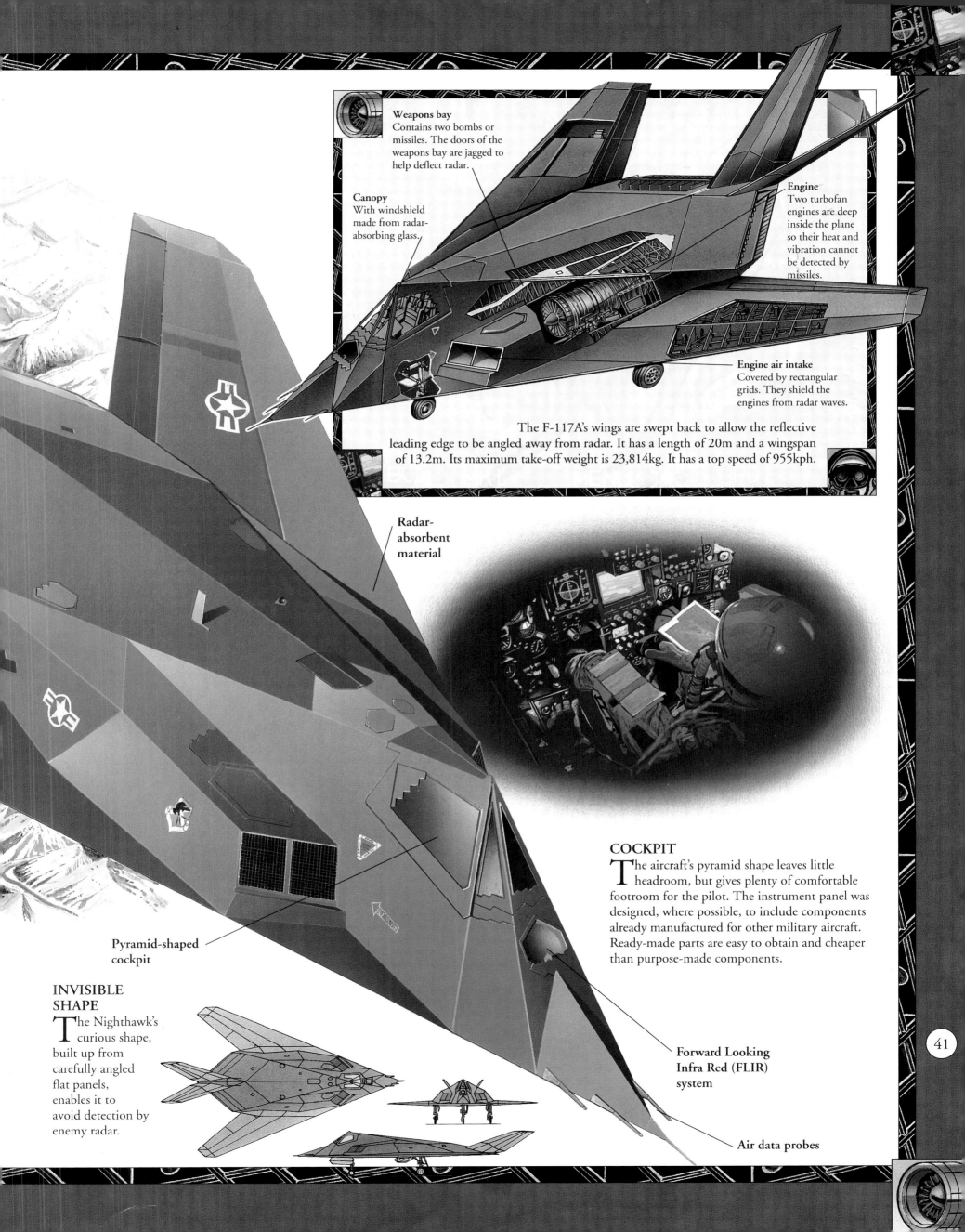

Weapons bay
Contains two bombs or missiles. The doors of the weapons bay are jagged to help deflect radar.

Canopy
With windshield made from radar-absorbing glass.

Engine
Two turbofan engines are deep inside the plane so their heat and vibration cannot be detected by missiles.

Engine air intake
Covered by rectangular grids. They shield the engines from radar waves.

The F-117A's wings are swept back to allow the reflective leading edge to be angled away from radar. It has a length of 20m and a wingspan of 13.2m. Its maximum take-off weight is 23,814kg. It has a top speed of 955kph.

Radar-absorbent material

COCKPIT
The aircraft's pyramid shape leaves little headroom, but gives plenty of comfortable footroom for the pilot. The instrument panel was designed, where possible, to include components already manufactured for other military aircraft. Ready-made parts are easy to obtain and cheaper than purpose-made components.

Pyramid-shaped cockpit

INVISIBLE SHAPE
The Nighthawk's curious shape, built up from carefully angled flat panels, enables it to avoid detection by enemy radar.

Forward Looking Infra Red (FLIR) system

Air data probes

Firebird

"No other aircraft can match it. It can race to a fire, scoop water from a nearby lake and "bomb" the fire with it up to 50 times over."

Louis Brennan,
fire-fighter and pilot

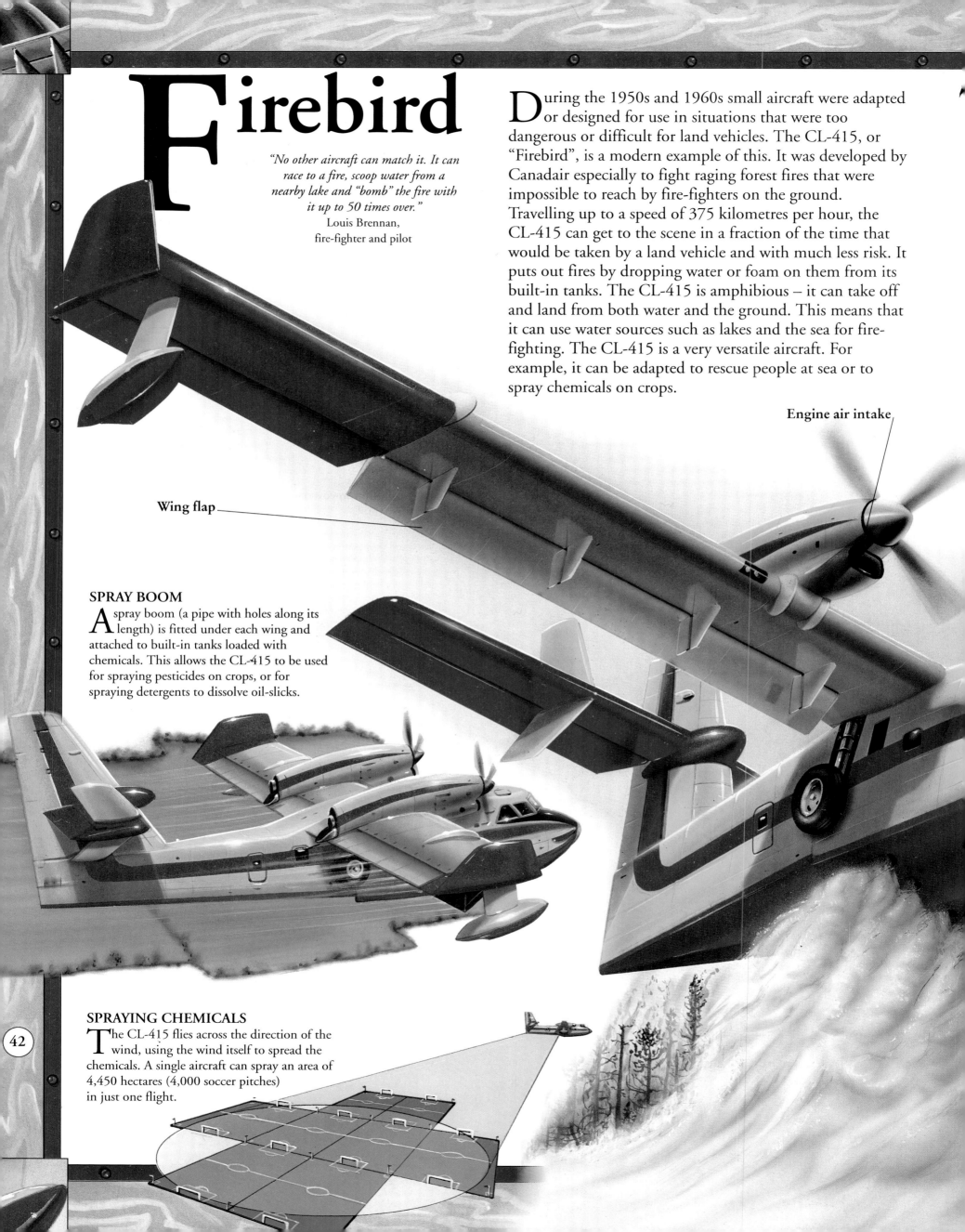

During the 1950s and 1960s small aircraft were adapted or designed for use in situations that were too dangerous or difficult for land vehicles. The CL-415, or "Firebird", is a modern example of this. It was developed by Canadair especially to fight raging forest fires that were impossible to reach by fire-fighters on the ground. Travelling up to a speed of 375 kilometres per hour, the CL-415 can get to the scene in a fraction of the time that would be taken by a land vehicle and with much less risk. It puts out fires by dropping water or foam on them from its built-in tanks. The CL-415 is amphibious – it can take off and land from both water and the ground. This means that it can use water sources such as lakes and the sea for fire-fighting. The CL-415 is a very versatile aircraft. For example, it can be adapted to rescue people at sea or to spray chemicals on crops.

Engine air intake

Wing flap

SPRAY BOOM

A spray boom (a pipe with holes along its length) is fitted under each wing and attached to built-in tanks loaded with chemicals. This allows the CL-415 to be used for spraying pesticides on crops, or for spraying detergents to dissolve oil-slicks.

SPRAYING CHEMICALS

The CL-415 flies across the direction of the wind, using the wind itself to spread the chemicals. A single aircraft can spray an area of 4,450 hectares (4,000 soccer pitches) in just one flight.

WATER TANKS

The CL-415 can scoop 6,130 litres of water into its tanks in 12 seconds. Foam is added to the water because it smothers the fire quickly and is therefore more effective than water alone. To drop the water and foam on the fire, the pilot opens doors in the bottom of the tanks using a control in the cockpit.

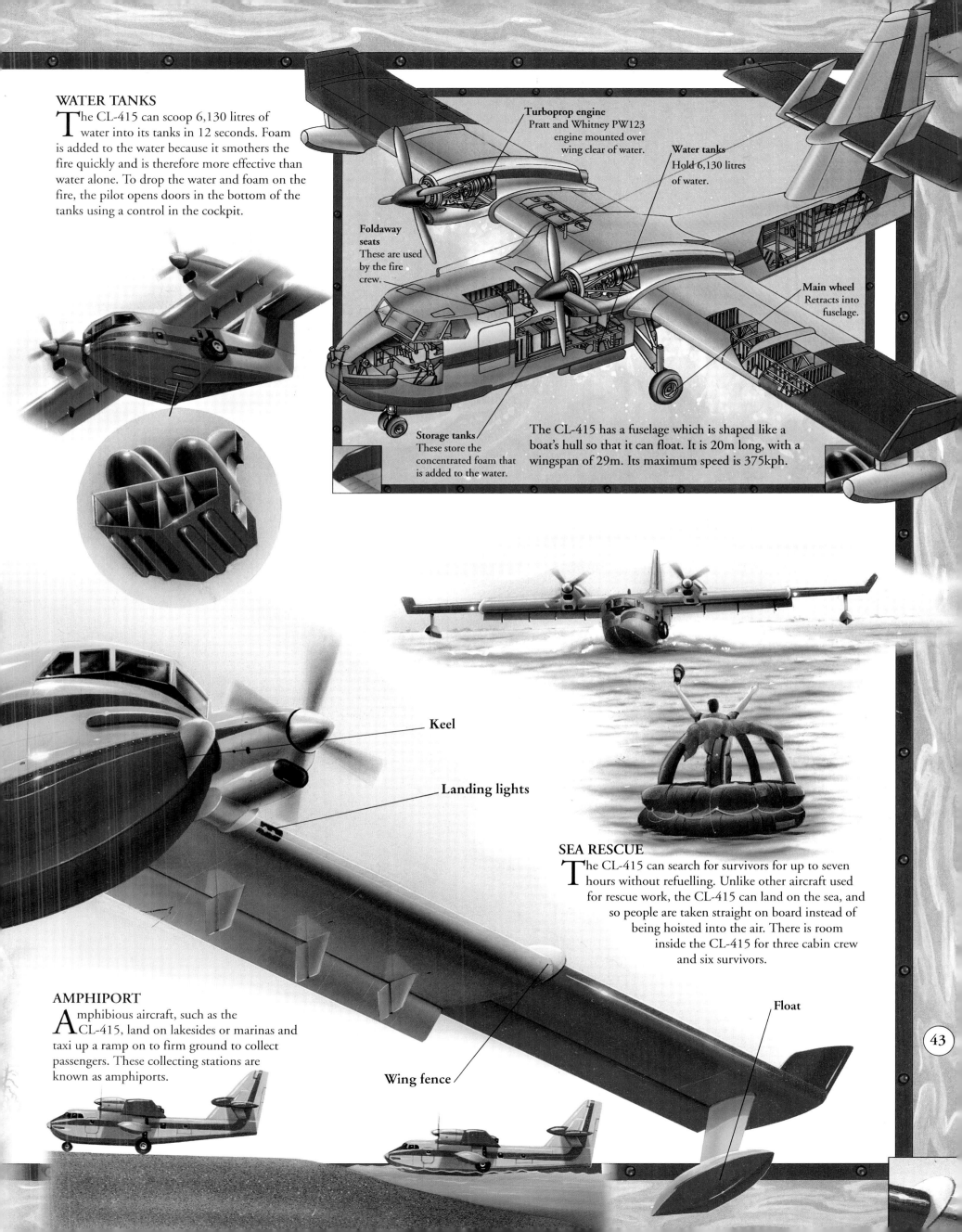

Turboprop engine
Pratt and Whitney PW123 engine mounted over wing clear of water.

Water tanks
Hold 6,130 litres of water.

Foldaway seats
These are used by the fire crew.

Main wheel
Retracts into fuselage.

Storage tanks
These store the concentrated foam that is added to the water.

The CL-415 has a fuselage which is shaped like a boat's hull so that it can float. It is 20m long, with a wingspan of 29m. Its maximum speed is 375kph.

Keel

Landing lights

SEA RESCUE

The CL-415 can search for survivors for up to seven hours without refuelling. Unlike other aircraft used for rescue work, the CL-415 can land on the sea, and so people are taken straight on board instead of being hoisted into the air. There is room inside the CL-415 for three cabin crew and six survivors.

AMPHIPORT

Amphibious aircraft, such as the CL-415, land on lakesides or marinas and taxi up a ramp on to firm ground to collect passengers. These collecting stations are known as amphiports.

Float

Wing fence

GLOSSARY

aerial photograph
A photograph taken of the ground or of objects in the air, by a camera carried on aircraft.

aerofoil
The special curved shape of an aeroplane wing or helicopter rotor blade. The aerofoil shape generates an upward force called lift.

aileron
A movable, hinged panel along the rear edge of each aeroplane wing. Ailerons swivel up or down. They always swivel in opposite directions. If one is up, the other is always down. Operating the ailerons makes the aeroplane roll to one side or the other.

airflow
The movement of air over and under a surface, such as a wing.

airliner
A large aeroplane designed specifically to carry passengers.

air pressure
The pushing force exerted on an object caused by the weight of all the air above it. Air pressure is greatest on the ground, at the lowest part of the atmosphere. Air thins out and its pressure drops with increasing height.

airship
An aircraft that rises into the air because it is lighter than air. An airship is constructed from a metal frame containing bags filled with hydrogen or helium gas. The pilot flies the craft from a gondola attached to the bottom of the airship.

altitude
An aircraft's altitude is its height above sea level.

amphibious aircraft
An aircraft that can take off from, and land on, either water or land. (Flying boats are not amphibious because they can operate from water but not from land.)

atmosphere
All the gases that surround the Earth.

biplane
An aircraft with two pairs of wings, one pair above the other. Biplanes were popular until the 1930s.

bomber
An aircraft designed to carry bombs.

bomb rack
A frame that holds bombs inside a bomber aircraft's bomb bay.

bracing wire
Tight wire stretched between a biplane's upper and lower wings and between the wings and the fuselage to hold the wings in place.

canopy
The clear, curved cover over an aircraft's cockpit. The canopy is usually made from a tough plastic called perspex.

ceiling
An aircraft's ceiling is the maximum height at which it can fly safely.

cockpit
The compartment at the front of an aircraft where the pilot and co-pilot sit. All of the flight controls are located in the cockpit.

console
The panel in front of the pilot containing the instruments used when flying.

cowling
A removable outer cover which is used to protect an engine.

cradle
Part of an early Wright Brothers' aeroplane. This is where the pilot lay, and from where he steered the aircraft.

cruise missile
A very accurate flying bomb. After it is fired from a ship or dropped from an aircraft, a cruise missile flies under the power of its own jet engine. It steers itself towards the target with pinpoint accuracy by comparing its view of the ground via a built-in television camera with a map stored in its computer memory.

cruising speed
An aircraft's cruising speed is the speed at which it normally flies.

cylinder
One of the chambers inside a piston engine where fuel and air are compressed and burned to provide power.

de-icing
The removal of ice from an aircraft while it is flying. In some weather conditions, ice can form on an aircraft's windows and wings. Ice building up on a wing's smooth curved shape can affect its ability to create the lifting force that keeps the plane in the air. An airliner's flight-deck windows are electrically heated and the leading edges of the wings are heated by air from the engines to prevent ice forming.

dogfight
A battle in the air at close quarters, between fighter planes. The planes twist and turn in the air at great speed in an attempt to train their guns on each other. The Sopwith Camels were particularly good at dogfighting.

drag
A force caused by air resistance that acts to slow an aircraft down.

elevator
A movable hinged panel along each rear edge of an aircraft's tail plane. When both strips swivel up, the plane tilts tail-down. When they swivel down, the tail is pushed up. Elevators make a plane soar or dive.

fighter
A small, fast and well-armed aircraft designed to find and attack other aircraft.

flap
A movable section at the back of a wing, extended backwards to generate more lift on take-off and before landing.

flight deck
The part at the front of an aircraft where the pilot and other crew sit. A flight deck is larger than a cockpit.

flight engineer
Aircraft used to be flown by a crew of three – the pilot, the co-pilot and the flight engineer. The flight engineer monitored the engines during a flight. Nowadays, computers normally monitor engines, so flight engineers are not needed. Concorde, however, still has a flight engineer.

fuselage
The body of an aircraft, running from nose to tail. The fuselage contains the cockpit or flight deck, the cargo hold and the passenger cabin.

galley
Another name for the kitchen or food preparation area in an aircraft.

glider
An aircraft without an engine. Gliders are towed into the air by a powered aircraft or by a tow-line attached to a winch on the ground, and soar higher on rising currents of air.

gondola
The crew compartment that hangs underneath an airship.

hub
The central part of a wheel or propeller.

hull
The watertight body of a boat, ship, submarine or flying boat.

hydraulic
Powered by the pressure of oil forced through pipes by a pump.

jet engine
An engine that uses a jet of gas to push an aircraft through the air. The jet is produced by sucking air into the front of the engine, compressing it and mixing it with burning fuel. This causes the air to expand rapidly, and it rushes out of the back of the engine as a powerful exhaust.

keel
The main structure along the base of a ship, flying boat or seaplane, on which the rest of the craft's frame is built.

leading edge
The front of a wing, tail fin or tail plane.

lift
The upward force on a wing, created by the airflow passing over it.

mach number
To measure the speed of a supersonic aircraft mach numbers are used. This is because the speed of sound is not the same everywhere in the atmosphere. Mach 1 is the speed of sound.

navigator
A crew member whose job was to plot an aircraft's course on long flights. After World War 2, navigation aids using radio and radar enabled pilots to keep their craft on course, and so navigators were no longer needed.

outrigger wheel
A small wheel at or near the end of an aircraft's wing, used to steady the aircraft and stop its wing-tips from touching the ground.

piston engine
An engine, similar to a car engine, that works by burning fuel inside cylinders. Hot gases push a piston down the cylinder to generate power to turn a propeller.

pitch
One of the three ways in which an aircraft can move. The other two are roll and yaw. Using the elevators in the tail to tilt the aircraft's nose up or down causes a change in pitch.

pre-flight checks
Checks made before take-off to ensure that the flaps are moving correctly, the engines are running smoothly and all the instruments are working properly.

pressure suit
Pilots of high-flying fighters, bombers and spyplanes wear a pressure suit. It inflates automatically like a balloon when the aircraft turns sharply, to stop blood draining away from the pilot's head into the legs. Pilots who fly at the highest level wear a pressure suit that looks like an astronaut's spacesuit. The suit, a helmet and gloves completely cover the pilot.

pressurised
When something is raised to a higher pressure than normal it is pressurised. The cabins in airliners are pressurised. Airliners fly at heights where the air is too thin for passengers to breathe, so the air pressure in the cabin is raised in order that passengers can breathe normally.

propeller
A set of thin, angled blades attached to a central hub. When the hub spins, the angled blades force air backwards, which pushes the aircraft forwards.

radar
A device used to detect the position of objects by measuring the echo of radio signals beamed at them. The letters of the word radar stand for RAdio Detection And Ranging.

radome
A dome-shaped cover made from a material through which radio waves can pass, used to protect radar equipment inside it.

rib
The parts of a wing's frame that run from the front of the wing to the back.

rivet
A metal peg used to hold two pieces of metal together. The process of fitting rivets is called riveting.

roll
One of the three ways in which an aircraft can move. The other two are pitch and yaw. Using the ailerons to raise one wing and lower the other makes an aircraft roll.

rotor
The rotating blades of a helicopter. Each rotor blade is like a long, thin wing. Most helicopters have two rotors, a larger main rotor on top to lift the craft into the air and a smaller rotor in the tail to stop the craft from spinning.

roundel
A circular identifying mark on an aircraft.

rudder
A swivelling panel in an aircraft's vertical tail fin. Turning the rudder makes the tail swing round to the left or right.

sight
A device used by the crew to aim a gun or to aim bombs at a target on the ground.

skids
A pair of long, thin runners fitted to the underside of a helicopter.

slat
A panel that extends from the front of the wing to make the wing bigger. This generates more lift so that the aircraft can land or take off more safely at low speeds.

sonic boom
When an aircraft flies faster than the speed of sound, the air in front of the aircraft is compressed so much that it forms a shock wave that travels out through the air and even reaches the ground. As the shock wave passes by, people hear it as a double bang called a sonic boom.

sortie
A mission flown by a military aircraft.

spar
Part of the frame inside a wing that supports the wing's weight. Spars are strong tubes or beams that lie along the length of wings, from wing-tip to wing-tip.

spoiler
A panel in the wing which can be raised to spoil the flow of air over the wing. Spoilers are used to slow an aircraft down and increase its rate of descent before landing.

stealth aircraft
A stealth aircraft is one designed so that it is difficult to detect by radar. It is carefully shaped so that radio waves that hit it are not reflected back from where they came. It is also covered with a special coating that absorbs radio waves and weakens the reflections.

supersonic
Faster than the speed of sound. The speed of sound changes when the air temperature changes. As the air is colder higher up in the atmosphere, the speed of sound changes also with height. At sea level, it is 1,225kph.

tail fin
The vertical part of an aircraft's tail. The rear part of the fin is hinged so that it can swivel, forming a rudder.

taxiing
An aircraft is taxiing when it is moving on the ground under its own power.

thrust
The force produced by a jet engine that pushes an aircraft along.

titanium
A metal used to build the fastest aircraft. Air rubbing against the outer skin of an aircraft heats the metal up. Most aircraft are made from aluminium, which melts at 660°C. An aluminium plane flying at three times the speed of sound would melt. Planes that fly this fast are made from titanium, which melts at 1,660°C. The Blackbird's fuselage is made from titanium.

torque
Twisting or turning caused by the rotation of blades, such as in a helicopter.

turbine
A wheel with angled blades. The turbine spins when a liquid or gas strikes the blades.

turboshaft engine
A type of jet engine used by helicopters. The jet of gas from the engine spins a turbine, which turns the rotor blades.

undercarriage
An aircraft's wheels – also known as landing gear.

variable pitch
The angle of an aircraft's propeller blades can be changed. This is known as variable pitch. Changing the angle of the blades increases or decreases the thrust produced by the propeller. One angle is best suited to slow flying speeds, another to fast cruising at high altitude.

wheelhouse
Large airships built in the 1930s were steered by turning large wheels. The cabin in which these wheels were located was called the wheelhouse.

wing fence
A vertical strip running from front to back on an aircraft wing. The wing fence is designed to improve the airflow over the wing so that it creates the maximum lift.

wing strut
A wooden or metal post that links the upper and lower wings of a biplane and holds them the correct distance apart.

wing-warping
The Wright Brothers used wing-warping to steer the first aircraft. The pilot pulled wires to bend the wing-tips and change the airflow over them.

yaw
One of the three ways in which an aircraft can move. The other two are pitch and roll. Turning the rudder causes the aircraft's nose to turn, or yaw, to the left or right.

INDEX